Architecture of Commonality
Grounds for Hope

Architecture of Commonality
Grounds for Hope

Edited by Tomà Berlanda

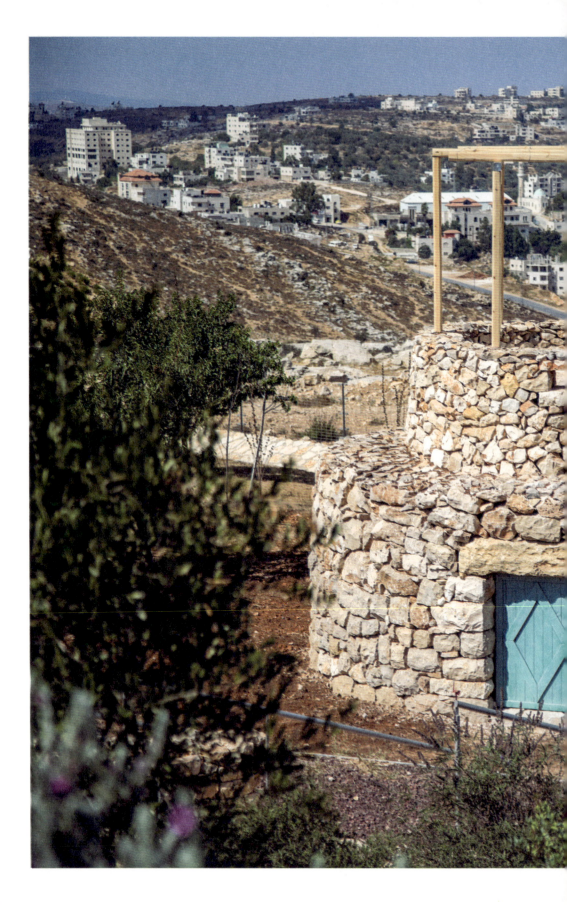

Table of Contents

16
Foreword
Farrokh Derakhshani

20
Editor's Note
Tomà Berlanda

24
Roots of Hope
Tomà Berlanda

WALKS

32
Building Arab Institutions: The Palestinian Museum in Regional Context
Amin Alsaden

50
Shaping Cultural Narratives: The Palestinian Museum in the Context of heneghan peng architects
Adrian Lahoud

60
The Palestinian Museum in the Time of the Chaotic Garden
Alexandre Kazerouni

72
Palestinian Walks
Raja Shehadeh

STONES

78
Palestinian Architecture and Stereotomy: Past and Present
Elias and Yousef Anastas in Conversation with Nadi Abusaada

94
Appreciation of the Landscape
Róisín Heneghan in Conversation with Cristina Steingräber

120
The Palestinian Museum
Hanan Toukan

SEEDS

138
Gardens in Dialogue
Lara Zureikat in Conversation with Walter J. Hood

154
The Land Knows You, Even When You Are Lost: Tuning In to Plants in Seven Acts
Mirna Bamieh

VOICES

172
Reflecting on the Institution
Adila Laïdi-Hanieh

176
Reflecting on the Aga Khan Award for Architecture for the Palestinian Museum
Meisa Batayneh

182
Reflecting on the Educational Programme at the Palestinian Museum
Sarah Zahran

188
Reflecting on the Garden Design
Lara Zureikat

194
The Birth of the Museum
Shadia Touqan
Beshara Doumani
Nabil Qaddumi
Omar Al-Qattan

216 Contributor Biographies
222 Acknowledgements
223 Image Credits
224 Imprint

Foreword
Farrokh Derakhshani

Culture is a basic need in every society, along with the other essential human needs for survival. As the most important vehicle for continuity and for connecting societies, culture appears in different forms: intangible manifestations across the arts, in literature, music, celebrations, rituals, lifestyles, and tangible testimonies such as artefacts and architecture. All of these together represent the identity of various societies and provide aspirations for their prosperity. Societies, by exchanging and learning from each other's culture(s), hope to find commonality between their values and ethics.

Architecture, because of its very nature, scale, and durability, plays a specific role, accommodating people's various activities and the housing structures they create. It facilitates the many functional needs of individuals and societies at large and, ideally, ensures the creation of physical environments that enhance the quality of life of its users. Amongst various building types, in more recent history 'museums' have been created as the centrepiece of celebrating our cultures, housing and displaying the visual realities of the past, not specifically of any particular society, but of a plurality of cultures, providing an environment for their evolution. Museums are also places to present the artistic manifestation of the present by showcasing aspirations for the future.

Yet, museums are not just frameworks for the display of objects, but are created to tell stories, real or imaginary, objective or subjective. The Palestinian Museum in Birzeit is no exception. It was conceived precisely as a place to tell the story of the people of a land over thousands of years, especially to the new generations. It is also a symbol for all those dispersed across the globe who belong to this shared culture. Because of its bold architectural expression and exceptional landscaping, the project received the Aga Khan Award for Architecture in 2019.

Stories nourish each society's identity and culture, giving ground to a commonality that needs to be considered, contested, reconciled, and, above all, shared. This commonality can also be described as the culmination of aspirations that each generation passes on to the next. The present volume tells some of the stories behind and around the creation of the Palestinian Museum, conveyed by scholars from different academic fields, in the hope that it will inspire more stories in the future.

The Aga Khan Award for Architecture, since its creation in 1977 by His Highness the Aga Khan, recognises every three years a number of recent architectural achievements most relevant to their time and context. Through a network of experts around the world, such exceptional projects, in service of Muslim societies, are selected by an independent master jury after a rigorous on-site review of the finalists. The Award tries to enhance the quality of life of societies by showcasing forward-looking projects that are rooted in their respective context and are able to stimulate a better future. To date, some 128 such projects have been honoured by the Award and presented to the world at large, five of them located in Palestine:

Restoration of the Dome of Al-Aqsa Mosque (1986), Rehabilitation of Hebron Old Town (1998), Old City of Jerusalem Revitalisation Programme (2004), Revitalisation of Birzeit Historic Centre (2013), and, in 2019, the Palestinian Museum became one of the six recipients of the 14th cycle of the Aga Khan Award for Architecture.

The extraordinary architectural solutions and the imaginative landscape of the project enjoyed the unanimous admiration of the Master Jury, which recognised the bold design, devoid of any nostalgia or mockery of traditional forms yet with landscaping that is rooted in the history of place. The project symbolises a potential site for celebrating the past and inspiring the future. Since its conception, the walls and the gardens of the Palestinian Museum have witnessed many events and activities, with many more to come – and each will create stories for the future.

Please scan the QR code to view the Aga Khan Award for Architecture film portraits of Restoration of the Dome of Al-Aqsa Mosque, Rehabilitation of Hebron Old Town, Old City of Jerusalem Revitalisation Programme, Revitalisation of Birzeit Historic Centre, and the Palestinian Museum.

Editor's Note
Tomà Berlanda

Architecture of Commonality: Grounds for Hope is an edited collection of essays by scholars, designers, and stakeholders that takes its cue from reflections on the Palestinian Museum in Birzeit, Palestine, one of the recipients of the Aga Khan Award for Architecture in 2019, to expand on the role of museums and cultural institutions in Palestine, and the Arab world.

The long history of the genesis of the museum as an institution is the framing device for a multiplicity of voices to reflect on the role that architecture plays in the orchestration of memorialisation, on the significance of curatorial strategies that respond to situations of conflict, and on a discussion of the blurred boundaries between architecture, landscape, and land art. Realising the polyhedric complexity of the work at hand, and the need to find languages able to speak across themes and disciplines, we invited contributors who are scholars, designers, activists, and institution-makers; and they also make their voices available in a video accessible through a dedicated QR code.

As a way to reflect on the deep ties the museum building and its gardens hold to the ground and the surrounding landscape, the collection of texts is structured around four main thematic sections: Walks, Stones, Seeds, and Voices. The intention is to move beyond the confines of each individual project – presenting insights on the role that cultural establishments play in planting seeds of hope for the future, while inviting readers to engage in conversations within the political and historical framework of Palestine and the region.

 Please scan the QR code to view the film about the Palestinian Museum.

WALKS

The journey starts with a series of 'Walks', with contributions by Amin Alsaden, Adrian Lahoud, and Alexandre Kazerouni. These Walks focus attention across borders, meandering through cultural institutions in the Middle East, a history of museums in Palestine, and culminate in a review of the trajectory of the architectural designers, with an emphasis on their interest in tying together topography, structure, and space. An excerpt from Raja Shehadeh's 'Palestinian Walks' brings readers into the realm of the metaphysical experiences that wandering, and the encounter with the landscape, allow in capturing meaning and symbolic values.

STONES

The section 'Stones' builds upon these foundational premises, featuring contributions by Nadi Abusaada in conversation with Elias and Yousef Anastas, and Cristina Steingräber in conversation with Róisín Heneghan. The different threads address the particular tradition of stone masonry and stereotomy in the region, together with the conceptual premise of the design strategy. Hanan Toukan's essay cements the framing, by meticulously annotating the steps and timeline that led to the official opening of the museum.

SEEDS

'Seeds' expands the register of conversations on the living nature of wild plants and the importance of growing food as part of planting seeds of resistance to occupation. This is done through contributions by Walter J. Hood in conversation with Lara Zureikat, as well as Mirna Bamieh's artistic observations, making clear how the terraced topography holds a central place in allowing for seeds of both physical and metaphorical hope to grow.

VOICES

Finally, 'Voices' concludes the journey of discovery into the museum with two different sections. One features interviews with various actors who were involved in the design, in the Aga Khan Award jury, and in the running of the institution and its educational projects: Adila Laïdi-Hanieh, Meisa Batayneh, Sarah Zahran, and Lara Zureikat. The other brings full circle the idea of contributing towards a history of the institution-making process, featuring inputs by Shadia Touqan, Beshara Doumani, Nabil Qaddumi, and Omar Al-Qattan, all of whom were involved in different capacities and stages in the momentous effort of laying the foundations for an architecture of commonality.

Conceptualised in early 2023, with the intent to promote scholarship on, and from, Palestine as a necessary step in offering meaningful hope for the future of us all, the book has purposely remained unaltered during the recrudescence of the conflict in the occupied Palestinian territories.

Traditional method of excavating the soil on the construction site for the terraces of the Palestinian Museum

Roots of Hope
Tomà Berlanda

Twenty-five years have lapsed since the presentation of the early concept for the Palestinian Museum. Since then, every phase of its realisation has spurred reflection on issues that hold relevance beyond the specific case: ranging from the modes in which architecture participates in the orchestration of the memorialisation, to the significance itself of the museum as an institution, to the questioning of conventional spatial categories and the boundaries between architecture, landscape, and land art, and to notions of architecture as built ground.

The initial intention of Tawoon, the association that initiated the project, was to create a Palestinian life and remembrance museum to commemorate the 50th anniversary of the Nakba, the catastrophic turning point in Palestinian history, after which 'a country and its people disappeared from maps and dictionaries'.[1]

Mindful of the risk that the symbolic exhibition of the Palestinian oppression and struggle could lend itself to a sort of museumification of an ongoing past, the promoters of the initiative later arrived at a different decision. Without giving up the idea of representing the Nakba as an event and a site of the Palestinian collective memory, they gave the institution the mission of operating as an agent of empowerment, capable of nurturing creativity and innovation above and beyond its function of preserving memory and history.

The vision hence shifted towards an architectural oeuvre that, still under the label of museum, could communicate Palestinian culture with a view to the future. It is a vision that can unleash the development of new initiatives and activities beyond the sole conservation of testimonies of the past, a concept which might also appear incongruous operating in a context under the daily risk of destruction.

As such, the museum is intended to take active part 'in decolonising the learned helplessness of the Palestinians and breaking their inflicted confinement',[2] contributing to the development of alternative political imaginaries.

The innovative potential of abandoning the traditional understanding of a museum as a container of artworks emerged during the Palestinian Museum opening in 2016, when the absence of objects on display, besides being an honest admission and denunciation of the challenging process of building a museum under military occupation, was proudly defined as being the true content of the exhibition. Absence, it was said, 'is the crucial feature of our Palestinian-ness ... a way of elevating a cause and a nation by saying it loud and clear: our absence itself is the object'.[3]

However, only few commentators recognised how the absence of a collection was not only the consequence of factual challenges, but also derived from having prioritised the construction of a transnational network able to reach and connect all Palestinians, both those living in the occupied territories and in the diaspora, above the accumulation of objects and the construction of a repository of artefacts.[4]

The international mainstream press instead obsessively focused its attention on the empty halls and walls, using them as a pretext to question how a museum can exist without a collection. An Israeli newspaper even went so far as to declare that 'there are no exhibits because there is no Palestinian culture'.[5]

After construction was completed, and most significantly after the museum received the Aga Khan Award for Architecture in 2019, the declarations of appreciation for the architectural excellence of the museum started to grow, and the building has become a paradigmatic example of a new way of conceptualising and designing museums.[6]

The unanimous consensus on building – with the physical qualities of its construction repeatedly defined as a beautiful and stunning artefact, as exemplary and impressive, and with the architects' ability to realise a perfect symbiosis between nature and culture admired – did not always go hand in hand with an analogue recognition of the relevance of the cultural project that the museum pursues.

This volume starts from the premise that the two ambits cannot be disjointed, and that the architectural and the societal projects from which the Palestinian Museum was borne are inseparable. Both are in fact crafted by the constructive aspiration of planting in the ground 'roots of hope'.

The word 'hope' is often used to define constructions conceived with the purpose of mitigating human suffering, thus contributing to the improvement of the material conditions of groups of underprivileged populations, or establishing places to address grief and painful memories. One generally speaks of a hospital of hope, a garden of hope, or a wall of hope. Even the museum has been celebrated as a symbol of hope[7] and a statement of optimism.[8] Yet in the superficial and rhetorical celebration of its symbolic value, one runs the risk of neglecting how hope, intended in the case of the Palestinian Museum not as a subjective state of mind but as rational choice of a people dispossessed of their historical narrative, can keep the alternative narrative alive, being the primary ingredient of the entire design trajectory.

Rather than hope in a generic sense, it is important to reference the concept of radical hope crafted by the philosopher Jonathan Lear, who posits that, in order to face cultural devastation, 'one must continue to see oneself as the person one has always been and still is as a part of the culture that used to be one's own'.[9] According to Lear, who studied the destruction of a Native American tribe as a prototype for cultural devastation, an attitude of radical hope is essential for life beyond mere survival, both for the individuals and for the communities to which they belong.

If the realisation of the museum is proof in itself of how the 'Indians of Palestine',[10] despite being the victim of systematic violence and despite an absence of rational justification for hope, are tenaciously capable of nurturing radical hope, then the adjective 'radical', which in a translated sense indicates a way of tackling a problem, digging deeply until the original elements emerge, is also a pertinent key to understanding the complexity of the expert work that allowed for the museum's concrete construction.

In a literal sense, radical connotes the system of roots of a tree, which grow, transform, and branch, and which, extending in depth, give stability to the soil and ensure the symbiotic connection between the plant and the earth.

The connection with the land has been appropriately indicated by many commentators as the generating principle of the project. Often, however, land and ground are used as if they were interchangeable synonyms. In the case of the Palestinian Museum, however, the choice of terms is crucial if one wishes to unpack the creative path followed by the designers.

Here, land should be understood not simply as territory on which the architects tested their ability to merge nature and culture and echo the landscape, but as both maker and marker of identity. In this sense, Palestine 'is not only a people but also a land',[11] and it is no accident that land, through the thematic lenses of erasure, fragmentation, distance, and belonging, is a recurrent protagonist of the exhibitions put on show, such as *Intimate Terrains: Representations of a Disappearing Landscape*.[12]

Ground is at the same time 'a palpable body and a mental construction',[13] and the term can be used to describe both the physical and tactile physicality of the superficial layer of the earth's crust, and the intersection of rational arguments on which a position is formulated. Taking this linguistic duplicity into account helps one to understand the implications of what Conor Sreenan, the project architect from heneghan peng architects, has described as being 'straightforward and simple' in terms of inspiration. 'It deals with facts on the ground, with the topography and geography of Palestine'.[14]

The facts on the ground to which Sreenan refers are more than the simple geometrical features of the site, its contours and orientation, but instead all the traces, physical and metaphorical, that make the site not a location but rather a repository of history. And topography is the tool which allows one to capture, record, and interpret these traces, and also to rewrite them. The ontological connection between the museum as a building artefact and its ground is one of topographic symbiosis. In other words, one can posit that the museum is an 'integrated incident in a coordinated cultural landscape'.[15] Rather than being embedded in the ground, it is truly a consolidate terrain from which narrations of experiences, interactions, and memories grow, like new branches from old roots.

The use of metaphors to describe the relationship between ground and construction is an exercise of limited significance if it is not supported by effective construction modalities.

The approach adopted by heneghan peng architects and Lara Zureikat of reading and interpreting the site, concretised in the skilful use of materials, mineral and vegetation, and of construction techniques, both innovative and traditional.

The richness of the project can be read by examining the section, the tool that best allows the confluence of 'the topographic qualities of both building and setting in the baseline, the horizon line and the profile line'.[16] Through the experience of the constructed site, and the movement along the contour lines in the garden, the visitor is brought to understand and experience how topography, literally the 'writing of place', holds a central place in Palestinian identity formation. This is true of the entire museum grounds. From the lowest point of the compound, where the access road enters the site, to the museum at the top of the hill, the landscape serves as a synthetic and strategic art form.

In this charged context, architecture carries intensified meaning and symbolism. All of which underscores the narrative and referential power of buildings, and the ethical and cultural role of architects and architecture.

Roots of hope for an architecture of commonality.

1. Elias Sanbar, 'Out of Place, Out of Time', *Mediterranean Historical Review* 16, no. 1 (2001), p. 87.
2. Yazid Anani and Hanah Toukan, 'On Delusion, Art, and Urban Desires in Palestine Today: An Interview with Yazid Anani', *The Arab Studies Journal* 22, no. 1 (2014), p. 211.
3. Fadi Kattan, 'The Museum Will Be without Objects', *The Funambulist* 6 (2016), https://thefunambulist.net/magazine/06-object-politics/museum-will-without-objects-karim-kattan.
4. Ali T. As'ad, '[Re]collection, [De]collection, and the People Curatorial: Calibrating the Preservation of Memory and the Dialectics of Loss in the Palestinian Museum', *Stedelijk Studies Journal* 11 (2022).
5. James Fraser, 'The Palestinian Museum Opened without Artefacts, but It's Still a Beacon of Hope', *The Conversation*, 2 June 2016.
6. See the chapter 'The Palestinian Museum, Birzeit, West Bank, Palestine,' in Laura Hourston Hanks, *New Museum Design* (London, 2021).
7. Oliver Wainwright, 'Palestine Museum Review: A Beacon of Optimism on a West Bank Hilltop', *The Guardian*, 17 May 2016.
8. Esther Hecht, 'Palestinian Museum by heneghan peng architects', *Architectural Record* (March 2017).
9. Allan Compton, 'Review of *Radical Hope: Ethics in the Face of Cultural Devastation* by Jonathan Lear', *American Imago* 65, no. 3 (2008), p. 489.
10. Appeared in *Liberation*, 8–9 May 1982. Republished in English translation as: Gilles Deleuze and Elias Sanbar, 'The Indians of Palestine', *Discourse: Journal for Theoretical Studies in Media and Culture* 20, no. 3 (1998).
11. Ibid. (1998), p. 26.
12. Hadani Ditmars, 'Landscape, Loss and Palestinian Identity: Intimate Terrains', Middle East Institute, 26 June 2019, https://www.mei.edu/publications/landscape-loss-and-palestinian-identity-intimate-terrains.
13. John Rajchman, *Constructions* (Cambridge, MA, 1997), p. 78.
14. Hadani Ditmars, 'Complex Geometry: Heneghan Peng's Palestinian Museum Takes Its Cue from a Natural Context', *Wallpaper*, 3 August 2016, https://www.wallpaper.com/architecture/heneghan-peng-designed-palestinian-museum-opens-in-birzeit.
15. Hanks, *New Museum Design*, p. 162.
16. Carol J. Burns, 'On Site: Architectural Preoccupations', in *Drawing, Building, Text: Essays in Architectural Theory*, ed. Andrea Kahn (New York, 1991), p. 154.

WALKS

Building Arab Institutions: The Palestinian Museum in Regional Context
Amin Alsaden

Figure 1. Exterior view of the Arab Museum of Modern Art

In 2010, while the Welfare Association was fundraising for its then prospective Palestinian Museum, another major cultural institution opened its doors in the region.[1] What came to be known as Mathaf: Arab Museum of Modern Art was inaugurated in December of that year in Qatar, with exhibitions celebrating its impressive collection, amassed over the preceding two decades (fig. 1).[2] Initially housed in two private residences, it was arguably not until the dedicated building – an existing school at the outskirts of Doha, repurposed by the French architect Jean-François Bodin – that Mathaf marked its official arrival.[3] The new venue was intended as a temporary home for this institution, a rather humble structure, and a far cry from the more ostentatious contemporary museum buildings being constructed around the world, and in Qatar itself.[4] Its design certainly pales in comparison to the exquisitely crafted Museum of Islamic Art in Doha by the Chinese-American architect I.M. Pei, which opened in 2008, or the dazzling National Museum of Qatar, completed in 2019 by the French Jean Nouvel[5] (figs. 2 and 3). But that did not matter, because it was the building that made the institution.

The genesis of the Palestinian Museum is different, and it operates within radically different conditions. When its new building opened in 2016, much was made in the media of the fact that it had no collection or inaugural exhibitions.[6] But several years later, that proved immaterial. The Birzeit institution took a divergent approach to its acquisition and curatorial strategies, gradually refining its exhibitions and programming offerings along the way. There was a realisation from day one that while museums usually construct buildings to house their collections and support their organisational structures, the Palestinian Museum could do things the other way around: build an institution with architecture.[7] Indeed, the significance of the building, designed by the Irish firm heneghan peng architects, goes beyond the design features, and beyond whether it is a fitting

Figure 2. Exterior view of the Museum of Islamic Art in Doha

home for a museum – notwithstanding the enormous symbolic weight of this specific museum, for Palestinians still living in their ancestral homeland, and for the displaced millions. The Palestinian Museum epitomises how architecture can make cultural institutions.

Today, museums are defined as institutions that serve the public, by caring for – and providing opportunities for reflecting on – a society's material culture and intangible heritage.[8] If that is the general mandate of museums, regardless of their specialisation, scale, or location, then buildings can be thought of as receptacles or vessels that safeguard and cultivate these multifold goals within their immediate communities, as well as catering for the countless international visitors who seek such institutions to learn about another culture. The majority of museums aspire to uphold these values, and use their architecture towards staging their contents, creating forums for meeting and exchanging ideas, as well as welcoming the public. The Palestinian Museum is no exception. However, the stakes are obviously higher when it comes to such an institution legitimising the Palestinians' claim to a sovereign nation, one consisting, at this point in time, of fragmented and contested territories – even though this museum is not sponsored by the State of Palestine (when, in fact, states tend to lead such initiatives, as museums are integral to the never-ending project of inculcating nationalism). Beyond the specific local circumstances, the Palestinian Museum and its building can be contextualised globally, and understood much more specifically in relation to its counterparts across the region too.

Situated within the current discourses and practices of how the discipline approaches cultural institutions, the Palestinian Museum exemplifies two salient tendencies. First, there is

Figure 3. Street view of the National Museum of Qatar

the 'Bilbao effect', a term coined after the Guggenheim lent its name to a new museum in the eponymous Spanish city.[9] This term describes a phenomenon whereby extravagant museum architecture is employed to give a city an instant facelift – presumably placing it on the global map, invigorating tourism, and driving economic progress.[10] The Guggenheim Bilbao Museum was not the first or only spectacular museum building in the modern era, but within a predominantly neoliberal and brand-conscious world, it became a popular formula. It was tried in myriad settings, with the expectation that architecture would be much more than a mere functional container.[11] Buildings must now provide an advantageous edge in a fiercely competitive planetary market economy, where even nationalism is commodified, in likeable snapshots of buildings often designed by imported, typically Western, architects. The Palestinian Museum's building might not be as large or hyperbolic in form, but it stands out as a remarkable object in its context, and it is inseparable from the ongoing modernisation taking place in Ramallah and adjacent Palestinian towns, like Birzeit. Second, and more broadly, the Palestinian Museum is part of the museum-building frenzy – the worldwide wave of construction activity to erect new museums, usually through architectural competitions.[12]

Aside from the global picture, however, it is the regional context of the Arab world that warrants closer examination. To use the word 'Arab' is not to assume an inherent or essentialising identity; any such totalising labels can be problematic, especially considering the striking plurality of the communities that constitute this part of the world, and its diasporas around the globe. But it is to speak of the strong cultural affinities across the Arab world, thanks to the Arabic language, linked histories, and shared living traditions – commonalities that cross national, linguistic, religious, and ethnic boundaries. It is also to underline the fact that, despite the borders imposed by Western colonising powers, and beyond specific contextual idiosyncrasies, there have been significant transnational entanglements throughout the region, considering factors such as intermarriage, education, and work-related movement. One of the distinguishing characteristics of this region is that it has always been a crossroads of cultural encounters, of endless exchanges and mobilities. Palestine, at the heart of this vast geography, has itself been a uniting factor over the past few decades: Palestinians have played a pivotal role in upholding the sentiments of pan-Arab collectivity, and their contributions to Arab countries, as expatriates, refugees, or new citizens, have been immense, although often unaccounted for.

Equally, the region shares a history of turmoil, with recent tribulations also creating a sense of solidarity between those affected by comparable adversities. The turbulence has been relentless: as one place appears to enjoy a period of relative stability, another falls into chaos. To candidly acknowledge this reality is to begin to understand the outlines of cultural developments in recent decades, and how they are intimately tied to geopolitical events – the art scene specifically, one could suggest, has been transformed by such events. It is no secret that there has been an explosive interest in the art and culture of the Arab world since the early 2000s, a decade marked by decisive regional events, especially the US-led invasion of Iraq, and its consequences. Entire collections of modern and contemporary art from the region have been assembled; international auction houses now have dedicated categories for 'Arab' (or 'Middle Eastern' or 'Islamic') art, fetching unprecedented prices; there is a demand for Arab artists both in the region and globally, in exhibitions at humble galleries, sizable museums, and large biennials; scholarship on the subject has expanded considerably, generating numerous symposia, research projects, and publications; and the number of both public and private cultural initiatives has proliferated.

A closer examination of this astonishing surge can reveal the outlines of a picture that will undoubtedly become clearer to future historians.[13] Some broad observations can be made at this juncture, by simply taking stock of the infrastructure being created to invigorate Arab art and culture across the region – especially the initiatives that transcend a strict focus on local contexts, aspiring instead towards forms of transnational collectivity (particularly when it comes to the Palestinian cause, which can often be situated within broader networks of support and solidarity). This may amount to an attempt at writing a history of the present, which is a risky endeavour, always conjectural and speculative, but which can also yield highly instructive revelations. Therefore, a geographical and chronological stroll can be helpful here – to account for the contemporary cultural landscape in the region, stopping by specific nodes to observe architecture's role in launching or consolidating institutions, and how geopolitics have largely shaped the infrastructure of this terrain.

While many dimensions of the region's cultural ecosystem are intangible, and thus difficult to quantify, the physical infrastructure is absolutely indispensable – especially the edifices that house institutions such as museums. One of the oldest contemporary institutions is Darat al Funun in Amman, an informal museum, with a permanent collection partially on display, and a year-round calendar of exhibitions and public programmes. Although launched in 1988, it was only in 1993 that this institution became a major contributor to Jordan's cultural scene, when it moved to its current home in Jabal al-Luweibdeh, a hill overlooking Amman's downtown. The site consists of several stone-constructed residences from the early twentieth century, renovated in the 1990s by the local architect Ammar Khammash, with Sahel AlHiyari adding some contemporary surgical interventions, like a boundary wall, a decade later (fig. 4). The institution continued to expand conscientiously, maintaining the character of the historical site, which also includes sixth-century Byzantine ruins, all nestled within a cascading landscape planted with

Figure 4. Westside exterior view of the Museum Darat al Funun in Amman

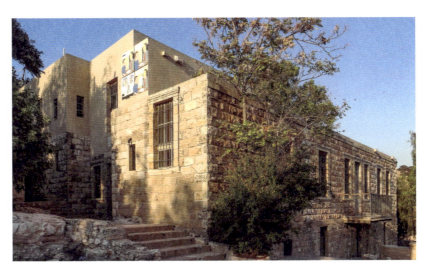

native and regional species.[14] Darat al Funun's architecture is unique, and so organically integrated into its site that it feels inconspicuous, camouflaged in its neighbourhood. Nonetheless, its architecture has become synonymous with the institution and its sensitive work, largely focused on Jordan and the Arab world.

Darat al Funun has also been known for its staunch commitment to the Palestinian cause, through exhibitions, public programmes, and residencies for artists and researchers, to name only a few of its initiatives. In fact, given its history of supporting Palestinian art and artists, this institution could be considered an integral part of the Palestinian cultural scene over the past few decades – until the establishment of institutions like the A.M. Qattan Foundation and the Palestinian Museum in Birzeit, and before newer ones like the Museum of the Palestinian People in Washington, DC, or the awaited Palestinian Museum of Modern and Contemporary Art in Paris, which started providing nurturing platforms outside Palestine.[15] Examples of important contributions include: Falastin al Hadara (The Civilisation of Palestine), a host of year-long shows and programmes celebrating Palestinian history and culture convened in 2017, on the centenary of the Balfour Declaration; a series of 2018 events, taking place across different Palestinian cities, including Gaza, Bethlehem, Jerusalem, and Ramallah, celebrating Darat al Funun's support of the Palestinian and broader Arab art scenes; and numerous solo exhibitions for prominent Palestinian artists such as Ahlam Shibli, Basma al-Sharif, Emily Jacir, Kamal Boullata, Khaled Hourani, Mona Hatoum, Nida Sinnokrot, and Samia Halaby.[16] The institution has also been at the forefront of knowledge dissemination about Palestinian and Arab art, through its publications, symposia, and fellowships.

While Darat al Funun has enjoyed greater longevity than most non-governmental institutions in the region, it was not the only one established during this period. Other institutions were founded soon after, with architecture always playing a decisive role. For instance, the A.M. Qattan Foundation was initially founded as a UK charity in 1993, with a branch operational in Palestine since 1998, making outstanding contributions towards reinforcing the vibrant local cultural scene. But it was two decades later – with its brand-new building, the polished headquarters designed by the Spanish firm Donaire Arquitectos – that this institution's activities coalesced in one place, declaring a permanent presence and a commitment to sustainable operations in Ramallah.[17] In the same city, which increasingly became the heart of Palestinian cultural life, the Khalil Sakakini Cultural Center was established in 1996, hosted in an early twentieth-century building renovated by the RIWAQ Centre for Architectural Conservation.[18] Although much smaller, the Sakakini has left an indelible mark in Ramallah and beyond, thanks to its community-oriented programmes. In the latter case, even more so than the Palestinian Museum, architecture created the institution.

Figure 5. Courtyard view of one of the restored vernacular buildings used by the Sharjah Art Foundation, with the Sharjah Art Museum seen in the background

In neighbouring Lebanon, Ashkal Alwan, The Lebanese Association for Plastic Arts, was founded in 1993, but it was only in 2011 that it moved into a former factory building in the Jisr el Wati area of Beirut, refurbished by Youssef Tohme Architects and Associates.[19] Entitled Home Workspace, the informal educational programme offered at the new venue created a strong association between this institution and the training of new artists, and experimental ways of displaying and convening around art. (Due to the economic crisis exacerbated by the devastating 2020 port explosion, Ashkal Alwan moved into a smaller space, renovated by Christian Zahr, in the Mar Mikhael neighbourhood; it remains to be seen how its new home will change the dynamics of this institution.[20]) In the same city, the Beirut Art Center was established in 2009, in another refurbished industrial building in Jisr el Wati, redesigned into a white cube space by the architect Raëd Abillama.[21] Other institutions, including several new museums, have been under development in Lebanon, but delayed due to ongoing political unrest.

Among the better-known Arab institutions originating in the 1990s is the Sharjah Art Museum in the United Arab Emirates, designed by the Dubai-based British firm Godwin Austen Johnson. Temporarily housed in a small restored vernacular building, the institution moved in 1997 to its purpose-built home at the core of old Sharjah, created to emulate traditional local architecture (fig. 5).[22] Since its inception, this institution has hosted some of the exhibitions of the Sharjah Biennial, founded in 1993, and one of the largest recurring art events in the region; the Sharjah Art Foundation, established in 2009, took over the biennial, working with other

Figure 6. Louvre Abu Dhabi by Ateliers Jean Nouvel

Figure 7. Grand Egyptian Museum by heneghan peng architects

Sharjah cultural organisations to offer year-round activities.[23] Spread across several venues in the city, with a conglomeration of buildings at the historical core, some of the Sharjah Art Foundation's buildings are restored, or even entirely rebuilt, vernacular or modern structures, while others are newly commissioned to meet specific needs; the institution has collaborated with various local and international architects on its projects, including the UAE-based firms dxb-lab, Shape Architecture Practice + Research, SpaceContinuum Design Studio, GAJ, and Dawson Architects, as well as the Peruvian firm 51-1 Arquitectos.[24] This model, which involves adapting existing buildings and operating across an extended landscape rather than focusing on a single centralised structure, is similar to that spearheaded by Darat al Funun, but clearly at a much bigger scale in the Gulf.

Creating new institutions housed in large iconic landmarks, however, has been the more common approach in the Gulf states, in an attempt to bolster the stature of their cities globally, while grappling with how the past might be reconciled with a drastically changing present.[25] In 2006 and 2007, Jean Nouvel and the British firm Foster + Partners were commissioned to design monumental buildings for the Louvre Abu Dhabi and Zayed National Museum, respectively; the government of the UAE had announced that these two will join other institutions housed in buildings by Canadian-American Frank Gehry, Japanese Tadao Ando, and Iraqi-British Zaha Hadid, among other internationally renowned architects, all for Saadiyat Island, just to the north of Abu Dhabi (fig. 6).[26] Architecture here is not only an apparatus for forging new institutions, but also a key ingredient in economic development, anchoring ambitious planning projects and making the city more competitive on the global stage (the panacea promised by the 'Bilbao effect'). In Dubai, cultural projects were planned at a slower pace than in Sharjah and Abu Dhabi, taking an in-between architectural approach. In 2017, the Dutch firm headed by Rem Koolhaas, Office for Metropolitan Architecture, completed a redesign of an existing warehouse, rebranding the venue as Concrete, Alserkal Avenue (Alserkal Initiatives had been founded a decade earlier).[27] The following year, 2018, the British firm Serie Architects completed the Jameel Arts Centre, a new but, by Dubai standards, understated complex.[28] Elsewhere in the Gulf, a number of other institutions are either being created, or relocated into new buildings – the most anticipated developments are those taking place in Saudi Arabia.

In North Africa, the creation of art and cultural institutions has been more sporadic, but there are a number of remarkable recent examples. Most art initiatives in this part of the Arab world have been relatively small private endeavours, but national museums have received more official attention. The same firm that designed the Palestinian Museum, heneghan peng architects, was announced in 2003 as the winner of the international competition to design the Grand Egyptian Museum, the world's largest museum of archaeological artefacts (fig. 7).[29] More than

Figure 8. Entrance of the Musée national du Bardo in Tunis by Codou-Hindley with Amira Nouira

two decades in the making, this new building upstages the older one housing the Egyptian Museum in Cairo, designed in the late nineteenth century by the French architect Marcel Dourgnon and considered the oldest museum in the modern Arab world.[30] Further west in the Maghreb, the Musée national du Bardo in Tunis was initially founded in a nineteenth-century traditional palace but underwent major renovation and expansion work starting in 2009, led by the French firm Codou-Hindley with the Tunisian architect Amira Nouira, completed a couple of years later; the considerably enlarged institution showcases millennia of Tunisia's material culture in one venue (fig. 8).[31] In Algeria, and occupying a building completed at the turn of the twentieth century by the French architect Henri Petit, but renovated and turned into a museum in 2007 by architect Halim Faïdi, is the Musée public national d'art moderne et contemporain d'Alger; the institution focuses on contemporary Algerian art, complementing the older Musée national des Beaux-Arts d'Alger, with its substantial collection of French and European art (fig. 9).[32]

Figure 9. Hall view of the Musée public national d'art moderne et contemporain d'Alger by Halim Faïdi

These are only a few representative examples, but there are many other institutions in this part of the world, each taking shape within specific circumstances. The founding of these institutions may have been determined by the personal choices of their founders, the priorities of governments, or the confluence of fortuitous conditions in various places, but they cannot possibly be isolated from the events that helped consolidate the roles of these institutions, both locally and regionally. Indeed, notwithstanding the contextual differences or the architectural features, when the milestones mentioned above are examined in tandem, certain patterns begin to emerge. It is not a coincidence, for instance, that many institutions were founded in the 1990s – the decade that started with the conclusion of the Gulf War, the Lebanese Civil War, the First Palestinian Intifada, and the Algerian civil conflict. The displacement of Palestinian and Iraqi artists and intellectuals during those years, escaping turmoil and longing for some freedom and stability in other Arab countries, inadvertently invigorated the cities where they took refuge, allowing certain institutions to prosper in ways that were not previously possible. The Oslo Accords of 1993 were followed by a hopeful period in the region as well, giving birth to several institutions in Palestine in particular – the seed for the Palestinian Museum itself was also planted in the 1990s.[33]

But two of the most decisive events, which had a profound impact on the cultural landscape in the Arab world, were the September 11 attack in 2001 and the concomitant 2003 US-led invasion of Iraq. That watershed moment in the early noughts created tremendous challenges for the populations of this region, not to mention Arabs and Muslims everywhere.[34] Some have argued that the changes – including the ensuing chaos, as well as new cultural policies – were part of the transformations purposely ushered in by the United States and its allies, in a plan dubbed the 'Greater Middle East' (or the 'New Middle East').[35] Culminating in the 'Arab Spring', the decade created momentous shifts within the art and cultural scenes, and these cataclysmic events generated considerable curiosity about the region and its populations, within a globalised world discontented with former Orientalist tropes. This led to the creation of a slew of new institutions invested in responding to the new interest, which also facilitated the flow of international funding, supporting various initiatives within and about the Arab world, including developments beyond its borders. Major renovations and relaunches took place, of entire specialist departments at international museums, such as the Louvre and Musée de l'institut du monde arabe in Paris, The Metropolitan Museum of Art in New York, and the Victoria and Albert Museum and the British Museum in London (most continued to engage with what is called 'Islamic' art, while updating their permanent collections and temporary exhibitions with works by contemporary Arab artists). It also meant brand-new institutions, such as The Mosaic Rooms, stewarded by the A. M. Qattan Foundation in 2009, in a London residence refurbished by Markam Associates.[36]

In addition, this included plenty of new institutions in the region itself, such as the ones mentioned above. These platforms now constitute the contemporary artistic and cultural infrastructure of the Arab world. It is important to deliberately use the word infrastructure, to underline that these institutions are as physical as they are organisational. Through such a brief survey of the new built form, one can begin to appreciate the undercurrents – yet to be fully investigated, but which beg to be acknowledged – that attest to how this infrastructure has been figuratively and literally constructed as a result of the specific geopolitics in this part of the world. What unites these platforms is not only the fact that they emerged in the aftermath of major events, but also a larger regional background, and how they exist within a geography that continues to grapple with the violent legacies of colonialism, the insidious mechanisms of today's imperialism, the totalitarian military or theological regimes, and various unresolved conflicts – while its communities attempt to find ways of housing their countries' historical artefacts, continue to produce and share meaningful creative output, and search for ways of representing their diverse cultures.

The larger dynamics aside, this brisk walkthrough across the institutional landscape of the region equally illuminates how architecture has been essential in making new cultural institutions like museums, and in affirming the role of existing ones, at political, societal, and urban levels. This transcends the basic expectation that buildings should primarily perform as suitable grounds for accommodating collection displays or curatorial visions. Museum buildings are also often meant to embody, or facilitate, a narrative to be experienced by visitors; their architecture is intended to communicate a public message, and negotiate between the communities (usually in the plural) they serve and their contents; in many contexts, these buildings host public space, where vital ideas are debated; buildings are supposed to bridge the present moment with the history of the place, and somehow anticipate how its cultures are moving into the future; and buildings are meant to be educational venues, informal schools of sorts, having a grander mission, some would argue civilisational, that speaks to collective ideals.

But this is not to glorify architecture as a universal solution, nor to prescribe buildings as tools for those wishing to create ad hoc public institutions. Built form on its own does very little, and can be a colossal waste of resources if not coupled with responsible organisational structures and a tight relationship with the communities being served. It is, however – to highlight the role of architecture in inspiring confidence – sheltering even fledgling or barely supported initiatives and providing groups with places to convene and exchange ideas. Buildings can be essential incubators, although they do not sustain cultural life on their own. The role of architecture, ironically, becomes clearer wherever it does not exist, or when it is heavily compromised. This was the case with the Kuwait National Museum, designed by the French architect Michel Écochard, and destroyed in 1990 during the Iraqi invasion; the building was restored, but the

Figure 10. Bottom view of the roof structure of the Kuwait National Museum by Michel Écochard

institution faltered after its structure was destabilised (fig. 10).[37] In Baghdad, the Iraq Museum, designed by the German architect Werner March, suffered the turmoil that followed the US-led invasion of the country in 2003; it remained closed until 2015, when the building was rehabilitated and reopened to the public after some of the looted artefacts had been retrieved, but it is still unable to serve a society in desperate need for such institutions.[38]

The Palestinian Museum, therefore, is far from an odd exception or regional anomaly, even though one must always be cognisant of the extreme challenges of its context, and equally concede to the fact that this is an institution that is still evolving. It has a long way to go until it builds a collection – if that is deemed the right strategy for the institution – or devises a resilient curatorial vision that can adapt to the precarity of the local situation, and embed itself within various communities to sustain its operations in the long run.[39] However, as a new museum, it is a typical product of ongoing global practices, part of the proliferation of museum buildings worldwide, which is giving shape to new institutions or providing extensions to existing ones. More specifically, the Palestinian Museum is a natural development in the Arab world, where architecture has been instrumental in asserting the arrival of new institutions, despite the great challenges the region continues to face.

I am grateful to Adila Laïdi-Hanieh and Tomà Berlanda for the invitation to contribute to this volume. I also thank Cristina Steingräber, Ella Neumaier, Nadia Siméon for their support, and Dawn Michelle d'Atri for her thoughtful editing of my text.

1   In 2010, a year before the architects were selected in an international competition, the Welfare Association announced that it had raised US$2 million for the Palestinian Museum project. See Nabil Hani Qaddumi, 'Message from the Chairman', in Welfare Association, *2010 Annual Report: Commitment Continues*, 2010, https://www.taawon.org/sites/default/files/AR2010_English.pdf.

2   'Qatar Museums Authority announces the opening, Mathaf: Arab Museum of Modern Art', *e-flux Announcements*, 16 December 2010, https://www.e-flux.com/announcements/36108/qatar-museums-authority-announces-the-opening.

3   'About Us', Qatar Museums: Mathaf, https://mathaf.org.qa/en/about-us.

4   I am not exploring here the alignments, or lack thereof, between the architecture and contents of, or the politics behind, these new developments. Soon after the inauguration of the Mathaf building, criticism was levelled against Qatar's motives behind constructing these new museums. For example, see Nicolai Hartvig, 'Qatar Looks to Balance Its Arts Scene', 6 January 2012, *The New York Times*, https://www.nytimes.com/2012/01/07/arts/07iht-scdoha07.html; and Rooksana Hossenally, 'Qatar's Royal Patronage of the Arts: Glittering but Empty', *The New York Times*, 29 February 2012, https://www.nytimes.com/2012/03/01/world/middleeast/qatars-royal-patronage-of-the-arts-glittering-but-empty.html.

5   'Museum of Islamic Art', I.M. Pei Foundation, https://impeifoundation.org/works/museum-of-islamic-art; and 'National Museum of Qatar', Ateliers Jean Nouvel, http://www.jeannouvel.com/en/projects/musee-national-du-qatar.

6   Various news outlets seemed to relish repeating this fact in their headlines. See for example: James Glanz and Rami Nazzal, 'Palestinian Museum Prepares to Open, Minus Exhibitions', *The New York Times*, 16 May 2016, https://www.nytimes.com/2016/05/17/world/middleeast/palestinian-museum-birzeit-west-bank.html; 'New Palestinian museum opens without exhibits', *BBC*, 18 May 2016, https://www.bbc.com/news/world-middle-east-36322756; and Jonathan Ferziger and Fadwa Hodali, 'Abbas Opens Empty $24 Million Palestinian Museum in West Bank', *Bloomberg*, 18 May 2016, https://www.bloomberg.com/news/articles/2016-05-18/abbas-opens-24-million-palestinian-museum-on-west-bank-hillside.

7   Omar Al-Qattan had stated at the opening: 'Some institutions build a shell around their existing collections. We decided to build the institution first.' Quoted in William Booth, 'Palestinian museum opening without exhibits, but creators say that's no big deal', *The Washington Post*, 18 May 2016, https://www.washingtonpost.com/world/middle_east/palestinian-museum-opening-without-exhibits-but-creators-say-thats-no-big-deal/2016/05/18/c3f671d2-1c57-11e6-82c2-a7dcb313287d_story.html.

8   The latest definition, adopted in 2022 by museums from around the world, is summarised in these lines: 'A museum is a not-for-profit, permanent institution in the service of society that researches, collects, conserves, interprets and exhibits tangible and intangible heritage. Open to the public, accessible and inclusive, museums foster diversity and sustainability. They operate and communicate ethically, professionally and with the participation of communities, offering varied experiences for education, enjoyment, reflection and knowledge sharing.' See 'Museum Definition', International Council of Museums (ICOM), https://icom.museum/en/resources/standards-guidelines/museum-definition.

9   It is unclear who exactly coined the term 'Bilbao effect', but it was already quite popular in the late 1990s. The term is attributed to the writer Jonathan Meades, who is extremely critical of Gehry's design and what it stands for, and ironically suggests there is no 'effect' as such. See Jonathan Meades, 'The Bilbao effect', *The Spectator*, 21 October 2017, https://www.spectator.co.uk/article/the-bilbao-effect.

10 In retrospect, however, observers have argued that the Guggenheim Bilbao Museum was born out of the confluence of highly specific circumstances – which have often failed to be replicated elsewhere – and that the 'Bilbao effect' has been a misleading exaggeration. See Rowan Moore, 'The Bilbao effect: How Frank Gehry's Guggenheim started a global craze', *The Guardian*, 1 October 2017, https://www.theguardian.com/artanddesign/2017/oct/01/bilbao-effect-frank-gehry-guggenheim-global-craze; and Edwin Heathcote, 'Is the Bilbao effect over?', *Apollo*, 27 February 2017, https://www.apollo-magazine.com/is-the-bilbao-effect-over-guggenheim.

11 There have been some arguments, however, that suggest an understanding of function that transcends mere practicality, or that a museum's sole purpose should be to serve the content it is meant to present. How the museum might serve the city economically, or meet its patrons' desires, is an equally significant function, as long as that does not compromise the experience of the interior. See Larry Shiner, 'On Aesthetics and Function in Architecture: The Case of the "Spectacle" Art Museum', *The Journal of Aesthetics and Art Criticism* 69, no. 1 (Winter 2011), pp. 31–41.

12 By 2012, when the Palestinian Museum design was being developed, a new survey was published, accounting for over 600 museums and extensions constructed since 2005, most of which are dedicated to art, followed by history museums. See Lorena Muñoz-Alonso, 'Who's Leading the Museum Building Craze?', *Artnet*, 13 November 2014, https://news.artnet.com/art-world/whos-leading-the-museum-building-craze-165875.

13 I am grateful to have been able to conduct research on this recent history. I presented the first iteration of my findings as an installation at Darat al Funun, Amman, 2018, tracing three decades of contemporary art developments in the Arab world.

14 'Our Story', Darat al Funun – The Khalid Shoman Foundation, https://daratalfunun.org/?page_id=85; and 'Architecture', Darat al Funun – The Khalid Shoman Foundation, https://daratalfunun.org/?page_id=33.

15 The latter institution is apparently being developed between UNESCO and the Institut du monde arabe. See 'A Palestinian Museum', Institut du monde arabe, https://www.imarabe.org/en/exhibitions/a-palestinian-museum; and Nora Ounnas Leroy, 'Where is the Palestinian National Museum of Modern and Contemporary Art?', *The Markaz Review*, 12 December 2022, https://themarkaz.org/where-is-the-palestinian-national-museum-of-modern-and-contemporary-art.

16 In addition to browsing past programming on the institution's website, see 'Falastin al Hadara', Darat al Funun – The Khalid Shoman Foundation, https://daratalfunun.org/?event=falastin-al-hadara; and 'There Is A Light That Never Goes Out: Darat al Funun From Amman to Palestine', Darat al Funun – The Khalid Shoman Foundation, https://daratalfunun.org/?event=light-never-goes.

17 'About the Foundation', A. M. Qattan Foundation, http://qattanfoundation.org/en/qattan/about/about; 'Donaire Arquitectos Wins Best Architecture Design for AMQF New Building', A. M. Qattan Foundation, http://qattanfoundation.org/en/qattan/media/news/donaire-arquitectos-wins-best-architecture-design-amqf-new-building; 'The A. M. Qattan Foundation Building', A. M. Qattan Foundation, http://qattanfoundation.org/en/qattan/facilities/main-building; and Oliver Wainwright, '"Beacon of culture": West Bank's £16m arts centre opens against huge odds', *The Guardian*, 29 June 2018, https://www.theguardian.com/artanddesign/2018/jun/29/a-beacon-of-culture-west-bank-new-arts-centre-built-on-hope.

18 'About', Khalil Sakakini Cultural Center, https://sakakini.org/about/?lang=en; and Khaldun Bshara and Nazmi Jubeh, eds., *Ram Allah: 'Imarah w'Tarikh* [Ramallah: Architecture and History] (Ramallah: RIWAQ, Centre for Architectural Conservation and The Institute of Jerusalem Studies, 2002).

19 'About Us', Ashkal Alwan, https://www.ashkalalwan.org/about.php; and 'Home Workspace Public Opening', Ashkal Alwan, https://www.ashkalalwan.org/program.php?category=4&id=120.

20 Jim Quilty, 'Ashkal Alwan brings new forms and colors to Mar Mikhael', *L'Orient Today*, 27 July 2022, https://today.lorientlejour.com/article/1306910/ashkal-alwan-brings-new-forms-and-colors-to-mar-mikhael.html; and 'Project: Ashkal Alwan exhibition space', Christian Zahr Architecture Landscape Design, http://www.christianzahr.com/ashkal-alwan-project-space-architecture/5n61mrdnrwnoqi63ll3ol0ztc7jn2w.

21 'About', Beirut Art Center, https://beirutartcenter.org/about; and 'Beirut Art Center', *Nafas Art Magazine*, January 2009, https://universes.art/en/nafas/articles/2009/beirut-art-center.

22 'About The Museum', Sharjah Art Museum, https://www.sharjahartmuseum.ae/About-Us-(1).aspx; 'Sharjah Art Museum', *Universes in Universe*, https://universes.art/en/art-destinations/sharjah/art-spaces/sharjah-art-museum#c65989; and Sultan Sooud Al-Qassemi, 'Sharjah Art Museum: The Bellwether of Gulf Art Museums', *Medium*, 15 December 2016, https://medium.com/@SultanAlQassemi/sharjah-art-museum-the-bellwether-of-gulf-art-museums-abbed7692d41.

23 'About Sharjah Biennial', Sharjah Art Foundation, https://sharjahart.org/biennial-15/about; 'Mission and History', Sharjah Art Foundation, https://sharjahart.org/sharjah-art-foundation/about/mission-and-history; and 'Sharjah Biennial',

Biennial Foundation, https://www.biennialfoundation.org/biennials/sharjah-biennial/.

24 While the institution does not mention those responsible for designing its venues, various information can be found through other sources. See 'Sharjah Art Foundation Venues, Sites and Architecture', Sharjah Art Foundation, https://sharjahart.org/sharjah-art-foundation/about/sharjah-art-foundation-venues; 'SAF Architecture Backgrounder', Resnicow and Associates, https://resnicow.com/sites/default/files/saf_architecture_backgrounder.pdf; 'Sharjah Arts Foundation', Architizer, https://architizer.com/projects/sharjah-arts-foundation; and 'Sharjah Arts Foundation', Dawson Architects, https://dawson-architects.com/index.php/sharjah-arts-foundation.

25 Observers have argued that Gulf museums attempt to create distinctive designs, where architecture is almost more important than the content, in order to reconcile the need to define local identities informed by traditions, and out of a desire for international recognition. See Sarina Wakefield, 'Museum Development in the Gulf: Narrative and Architecture', *Architectural Design* 85, no. 1 (January 2015), pp. 20–27; and Roberto Fabbri, 'The Contextual Linkage: Visual Metaphors and Analogies in Recent Gulf Museums' Architecture', *The Journal of Architecture* 27, nos. 2–3 (2022), pp. 372–97.

26 'Louvre Abu Dhabi', Ateliers Jean Nouvel, http://www.jeannouvel.com/en/projects/louvre-abou-dhabi-3; 'Zayed National Museum', Foster + Partners, https://www.fosterandpartners.com/projects/zayed-national-museum; and 'Saadiyat Island Home to Guggenheim and Louvre Museums', Embassy of the United Arab Emirates, Washington, DC, 8 January 2009, https://www.uae-embassy.org/news/saadiyat-island-home-guggenheim-and-louvre-museums.

27 'Concrete at Alserkal Avenue', OMA, https://www.oma.com/projects/concrete-at-alserkal-avenue; 'Concrete', Alserkal, https://alserkal.online/venue/concrete; and 'Our Story', Alserkal, https://alserkal.online/our-story.

28 'The Building', Jameel Arts Centre, https://jameelartscentre.org/about/architecture-gardens.

29 'About The Grand Egyptian Museum', Grand Egyptian Museum, https://grandegyptianmuseum.org/about.

30 'The Egyptian Museum', Ministry of Tourism and Antiquities, https://egymonuments.gov.eg/en/museums/egyptian-museum; and 'Egyptian Museum in Cairo', World Heritage Convention, https://whc.unesco.org/en/tentativelists/6511.

31 'Architecture', The National Bardo Museum, http://www.bardomuseum.tn/index.php?option=com_content&view=article&id=60&Itemid=68&lang=en; and 'The expansion and renovation of the museum', The National Bardo Museum, http://www.bardomuseum.tn/index.php?option=com_content&view=article&id=182&Itemid=95&lang=en.

32 'Histoire du bâtiment', Musée public national d'art moderne et contemporain d'Alger, https://www.mama-dz.com/musee/histoire.

33 The Welfare Association was formally registered as a charity in 1993, and in 1997 its members arrived at the idea of establishing the Palestinian Museum. See 'Who we are', The Welfare Association, https://www.welfareassociation.org.uk/who-we-are; and 'The Museum', The Palestinian Museum, https://www.palmuseum.org/about/the-building-2#ad-image-thumb-1914.

34 A cultural institution, the Arab American National Museum, which opened in 2005, helped to dispel some of the misconceptions about Arabs and Muslims, particularly in the United States, at a time of pervasive negative portrayal. See Janice Ann Freij, 'The Arab American National Museum: Cultural Competency Training in Post-9/11 America', *The Journal of Museum Education* 36, no. 1 (Spring 2011), pp. 19–28; and 'About the Arab American National Museum', Arab American National Museum, https://arabamericanmuseum.org/about.

35 'The Greater Middle East Initiative', Aljazeera, 20 May 2004, https://www.aljazeera.com/news/2004/5/20/the-greater-middle-east-initiative; and Jumana Al Tamimi, 'The "New Middle East" and its "constructive chaos"', *Gulf News*, 10 August 2013, https://gulfnews.com/world/americas/the-new-middle-east-and-its-constructive-chaos-1.1218872.

36 'About The Mosaic Rooms', The Mosaic Rooms, https://mosaicrooms.org/about-mosaic-rooms-2; 'The Future Rewound & The Cabinet of Souls', The Mosaic Rooms, https://mosaicrooms.org/event/the-future-rewound-the-cabinet-of-souls; and Omar Al-Qattan and Marwan Jamal (Markam Associates), email messages to the author, 14 August 2023.

37 'Kuwait National Museum History', Kuwait National Museum, https://kuwaitnationalmuseum.weebly.com/the-history-of-the-museum.html; and Sundus Al-Rashid, 'Examining Kuwait's National Museum', The London School of Economics and Political Science, 7 April 2020, https://blogs.lse.ac.uk/mec/2020/04/07/examining-kuwaits-national-museum.

38 'About the Museum', The Iraq Museum, https://theiraqmuseum.com/pages/about-the-museum.html; and Angelica Villa, 'Iraq's National Museum Opens After Three-Year Hiatus', *Artnews*, 8 March 2022, https://www.artnews.com/art-news/news/iraqs-national-museum-opens-after-three-year-hiatus-1234621345.

39 In fact, there was a conscious rejection of assembling a collection for fear of 'harassment or confiscation by the Israelis', as stated by Omar Al-Qattan at the opening. Quoted in Oliver Wainwright, 'Palestine Museum review – a beacon of optimism on a West Bank hilltop', *The Guardian*, 17 May 2016, https://www.theguardian.com/artanddesign/2016/may/17/palestine-museum-review-ramallah-west-bank-israel.

Shaping Cultural Narratives: The Palestinian Museum in the Context of heneghan peng architects
Adrian Lahoud

In a relatively brief time, heneghan peng architects has produced a rich and exceptionally diverse series of cultural projects at remarkably different scales and in very different contexts. One of the largest museums in the world, the Grand Egyptian Museum in Giza (2003–present), designed to store the world's biggest collection of ancient Egyptian antiquities. The Giant's Causeway (2005–12), a visitors' centre located at a UNESCO World Heritage Site in Northern Ireland, shortlisted for an RIBA Stirling Prize. The Canadian Canoe Museum in Ontario (2016–19), a building meant to house and display the world's largest collection of canoes and kayaks, located alongside the waterway below the historical Peterborough Lift Lock. And the Palestinian Museum in Birzeit (2011–16), widely described as a 'platform for shaping and communicating knowledge about Palestinian history, society and culture'.

In all these projects, heneghan peng architects deploy design strategies that have become characteristic of the practice, drawing inspiration from topography and landscape, but also from local technologies and approaches to building, while navigating different institutional missions, curatorial strategies, and clients. Though we often speak of cultural buildings in general, attention to these specificities frequently reveals more differences than commonalities. The kinds of social diagrams embodied in museums are also changing, as collections become less important and public engagement and pedagogy take precedence. Tracking heneghan peng architects' work in the cultural sector is illustrative, both in terms of the consistencies towards design the practice evidences, but also the differences in procurement and mission that sit within the cultural ecosystem.

The most cited characteristic of heneghan peng architects' work is its relation to land form. Consider the four projects mentioned above. The Grand Egyptian Museum's grid fans out from sight lines established between the museum site and the Great Pyramid, the Pyramids of Khafre and Menkaure, in Giza. Located on the edge of the Giza Plateau and the Nile Valley, the Grand Egyptian Museum makes the most of the 50-metre-grade change between them to nestle the museum at this important threshold, constructing a new, artificial, and inhabitable edge. Originally intended to be crafted from steel and onyx in a pattern based on a Sierpiński triangle (with large equilateral triangles fractally subdivided into smaller and smaller ones), the proposed facade makes use of the iconography of the pyramid's triangular form to connect to the tessellated roof above – further emphasising the link to the context but also providing a clear structural logic for building set-out and construction. The Giant's Causeway, in turn, on the north coast of Northern Ireland, draws inspiration from the extraordinary geological history of the area. Made up of 40,000 hexagonal basalt columns, this unique coastline is the geological aftermath of a volcanic eruption that took place some 50 to 60 million years ago – leaving a crystalline, prismatic legacy that is considered one of the most important natural wonders in the United

Kingdom. Taking advantage of the grade change again, the project is partially buried. It rises to a premonitory-like point at its raised edge. The line of the cut in the folded form is composed of black basalt columns interspersed with glazing, clearly referencing the coastline. The Canadian Canoe Museum – unbuilt due to unforeseen site-contamination issues – is, like the Giant's Causeway visitors' centre, partially buried. It presents a single, curved facade that echoes the line of the waterway in the form of a new undulating contour on the site, creating a continuous, but richly differentiated relationship to the adjoining waterway. Finally, the Palestinian Museum, which is located on the precipice of a west-facing hill in Birzeit, north of Ramallah in the West Bank and adjacent to Birzeit University, takes a different approach altogether. The site for the museum falls away to the western edge, opening up to a broad valley and facing an opposing ridge that is now densely urbanised. heneghan peng architects chose to locate the building at the highest point of the site – on the top of the hill, in fact – despite the challenges this posed for phasing the project, which would have suggested a location further down the valley away from the edge. Unlike either the Giant's Causeway or the Canoe Museum, the Palestinian Museum asserts its presence at the top of the landscape. The monumental, object-like quality of the building is emphasised by its primary articulation: an angular, elongated triangulation of the west-facing facade with edges that touch at vertices as if to emphasise the abstraction of

Figure 1. Rendering of the waterway of the Canadian Canoe Museum in Ontario

Figure 2. Rendering of the triangular facade of the Grand Egyptian Museum in Giza

the geometry. Rather than extend the ground and have the building act as its continuation, in Birzeit, heneghan peng architects crown the site, introducing a new element at the top of the hill to clearly mark the institution's presence. The extrusions, tessellations, cuts, and folds that heneghan peng architects deploy to draw tectonic inspiration from the topography of the project's respective contexts are visible again here, but motivated by a wholly different geopolitical context and driven to different ends as a result.

What distinguishes heneghan peng architects' work from other practices inclined to draw formal tropes from landscape, however, is their approach to building materials and construction. Just as the formal logic of each project is careful to never elide, instead emphasising the artifice of the building's introduction into the landscape. Similarly, material choices and construction technologies take what is available, but they strive to push what is available beyond customary use in the pursuit of formal effects that tread a delicate balance between the matter-of-factness of the material and its abstraction.

In their competition entry for the Grand Egyptian Museum, heneghan peng architects' proposal included a kilometre-long free-standing wall acting as a facade made of onyx, a semi-translucent stone that is difficult to use in large planes owing to its brittle qualities. During initial studies, the quantities of onyx required at a large scale proved unfeasible and unable to cover the surface area of the enormous facade. The architects responded with a strategy to make use of smaller-scale panels, thereby reducing wastage, by subdividing the triangular facade into smaller and smaller triangular elements. The fractal-like effect of the facade is an

ingenious response to a limitation in the desired material, maintaining the consistency of the idea, but bending it towards a more achievable outcome – relatively speaking.

In the case of the Giant's Causeway, the importance of using basalt from Northern Ireland in a project designed to celebrate the unique basalt geography of the coastline proved similarly challenging because local basalt is very thin and unsuitable for load-bearing uses. In its early stages, the project sat within the remit of Ireland's Department of Heritage and Environment, which argued that the cost of building basalt columns was prohibitive and proposed cladding the columns with basalt tiles fixed to rails. When the project finally moved to the National Trust, the architects found ally in the client team; the architect Dawson Stelfox insisted that the project be built from local basalt, and the engineers Tim McFarlane and Francis Archer at ARUP proposed stacking the stones one on top of another and skewering them together with a steel rod threaded through their centres. Despite this, the strategy would generate a lot of wasted stones,

Figure 3. View of the Giant's Causeway visitors' centre in Northern Irland

so every basalt quarry in Northern Ireland fastidiously put large boulders to one side for two years until enough had been accumulated to complete the project.

In discussing the Palestinian Museum, Róisín Heneghan refers to the importance of stone construction in Palestine and the ubiquity of concrete, two materials that were integral to the project. Typically, in Palestine, stone is applied directly to concrete without a break or insulation. In the context of a project that aspired to high standards of environmental performance, both due to ambitions set out in the design brief and owing to interruptions in energy supply because of the occupation, the standard local method of stone and concrete construction would not be suitable. Moreover, the project brief made a clear requirement of ASHRAE standards for exhibition space to ensure that the museum was able to exhibit work by Palestinian artists and secure loans from international institutions, a situation that was already beset by challenges due to security concerns. That performance requirement exacerbated the need for improved environmental control, especially the insulation of the exhibition space. This drove a need to mechanically fix the stone to the concrete in order to create space to insulate the concrete and satisfy the performance requirements. In Palestine, mechanically fixing stone to concrete is uncommon; in fact, it is believed that only a single building in the West Bank had ever attempted it before. If the unfamiliarity of the construction technology were not difficult enough in this context, the winning competition entry depended on its monolithic appearance, eschewing the articulation of difference between the walls and roof such that the stone surface wrapped around the building seamlessly. That aesthetic choice added to the complexity of the construction, because joint alignment would need to be coordinated and aligned across the facades and the roof, meaning that rail set-outs would have to work backwards from the stone surface towards the concrete. With the support of the client and a determined contractor, the tolerances, joints, and set-out were completed correctly after a challenging start.

In each of the three projects described, and to various levels of success (for instance, the onyx facade was finally replaced by glass during a value engineering process in the case of the Grand Egyptian Museum), heneghan peng architects have attempted to intensify the topographical formal strategies with a clear tectonic relationship to material and construction that treats existing technologies and capacities within the construction sector as – in some important way – another site, which is to say a condition that depends on a close reading and analysis able to draw out latent potentials in order to better intensify spatial effects in the project. The consistency of approach to heneghan peng architects work belies its diversity because of this attention to the condition of the site and the conditions of the building's production. In the case of cultural buildings, however, a third dimension becomes a factor.

Collections, curatorial strategies, approaches to display and user experience, public engagement and public pedagogy are – to greater or lesser degrees – common concerns for cultural buildings. In the Gulf, the Arabian Peninsula, as well as in Lebanon, Jordan, and Palestine, there has been a well-documented surge in cultural investment that is creating a relatively diverse ecosystem of public and private institutions in a relatively short amount of time. From large-scale state-funded projects that aspire to a universality (or at least generality) in terms of the breadth of their collections, to projects that attempt to bring new coherence and insights to themes or periods poorly covered by other institutions, to precisely defined cultural projects built around specific locales or themes – these projects all embody certain kinds of shared characteristics, such as the desire to reclaim historiographic control over the narratives that surround cultural objects, usually by nations that only recently see that kind of aspiration as desirable or important.

Part of the reason for this is that such institutions are seen as part of the 'standard equipment' needed by the modern nation to edify their populations, to create global legitimacy and prestige. Post-Bilbao, many grand projects – such as Frank Gehry's Guggenheim and Jean Nouvel's Louvre Abu Dhabi, both on Saadiyat Island in the United Arab Emirates, Zayed National Museum by Foster + Partners, I.M. Pei's design for the Museum of Islamic Art, Jean Novuel's National Museum of Qatar, and Elemental's Art Mill, all in Doha, and heneghan peng architects' Grand Egyptian Museum – are on a geopolitical scale where the normalisation of relationships between states are lubricated by tourist flows and the art market. A second generation of museums takes a different route, not only in terms of their scale, but most importantly in their attempt to engage both local and international publics: museums such as the Barjeel Collection, the Jameel Arts Centre by Serie Architects, Alserkal Avenue, Jax district in Diriyah, and Ashkal Alwan in Lebanon, as well as forthcoming projects for a Contemporary Art Museum in Al-Ula, Saudi Arabia, organised around a collection of cultural objects from the Red, Arabian, and Mediterranean Seas by Lina Ghotmeh,

Figure 4. The large window fronts of the Palestinian Museum provide a vast view, combining architecture and landscape

or Asif Khan's Incense Road Museum itself organised around the historical importance of Al-Ula within the Incense Route. These kinds of categorisations are fraught, however. The cultural differences between the different contexts cited above should prevent us from rushing into too-easy generalisations, especially in any assessment of the architectural materialisation of these new institutions, without attending to the specificities of client, site, local expertise, et cetera, that do so much to shape the final project outcome. Architecture has an undeniable power to give form to these sometimes nebulous, oftentimes contradictory aspirations, frequently irrespective of the desires of the client or architect.

Institutional missions are always articulated with different degrees of clarity and purpose. Building procurement processes detail those processes in documents like design briefs, though frequently without considering how the shape of the institution evolves in interdependence with the spatial setting provided by the building. That is not a surprise, for the political economy of architecture is organised around a separation between building design and building delivery, with an even greater gulf separating institutional form from building form. For example, the 2,000-page design brief for the Grand Egyptian Museum was written by external consultants but with very little information about where artefacts would be displayed or how. Without a clear curatorial and display strategy, the project posed technical and creative challenges for the architects who had to modulate the spatial experience of a 490,000-square-metre building, six football pitches of exhibition space, while specifying floors able to take the load of an 83-ton red granite statue of Ramses the Great, rooms large enough to accommodate the 5,600 objects from the Tutankhamun collection, or fire management strategy around the exhibition of the Khufu ship or solar barge, a 43-metre-long vessel built in 2500 BC. The architects responded with a set of guidelines and zones that demarcated different categories of use within the building, but one senses a certain frustration at not being able to direct the visitors' attention or to shape the user experience around specific artefacts and sequences of display more carefully.

As set out in the architectural brief for the Palestinian Museum design competition, the winning design is conceived as a 'robust platform for shaping and communicating knowledge about Palestinian history, society and culture'. It intends to be 'the authoritative cultural voice for Palestinians worldwide'. The emergence of modern museums is bound up in the formation of the modern nation-state; they are an important part of the techniques that states deploy to create coherent historical narratives, narratives whose purpose is the production of subjects able to see themselves as both consumers and producers of that narrative. That ambition takes on a different character in the context of Palestine's occupation by Israel and its ongoing struggle for national self-determination. The design brief for the project is quite explicit on this point: 'For Palestinians to achieve self-determination, they must explain who they are, how they came to be, and their current conditions and aspirations.' Exactly who that explanation might be addressed to is an important question. On this point, the design brief for the project hedges its bets, pointing towards the local context, the need to engage communities, to build audiences and empower Palestinians in Palestine. On the other hand, it also clearly signals its intent to become part of a regional and international infrastructure of cultural institutions. That equivocation need not be resolved; indeed both ambitions can be mutually complementary. In many ways, this is exactly what the building has achieved in integrating the highest standard of exhibition space with a design strategy that consciously deploys interstitial spaces, edges, and excavations to create opportunities for institutional programming, whether through the terraced landscape that drapes down the valley from the building edge, to the amphitheatre for performance on its western elevation, or the elevated, wide, glazed corridor separating the amphitheatre outside from the gallery inside. In the affordances they provide, those spaces – conceived in dialogue with the inaugural director – embody a clear opportunity to create forms of institutional engagement and programming in relation to the local context that might not only fulfil the aspirations of the brief to engage with local contexts, but also connect those contexts to broader histories, including global ones. As in their work in Egypt, Canada, and Northern Ireland, the Palestinian Museum demonstrates heneghan peng architects' deft ability to create cultural resonance out of physical, social, and economic conditions – seeing how far the elasticity of the idea of a museum can be pushed in different contexts. Here in Palestine, they have achieved something arguably more important, and also posed a challenge back to the client in regard to the building programming, and therefore the site's porosity to the communities around it. If the work for the Grand Egyptian Museum sits within a space of relative geopolitical clarity – an Egyptian museum for Egyptian history as evidenced by Egyptian artefacts – projects like the one in Ireland or Canada present fewer complex challenges owing to the fixed nature of the collection in one case and the defined nature of the landscape in the other. In Palestine, neither the geopolitical context, nor the collection – not even the landscape itself – can be taken for granted. The building multiplies those ambiguities rather than diminishes them, and in doing so it retains the complexity of the context – physical, social, institutional.

The Palestinian Museum in the Time of the Chaotic Garden
Alexandre Kazerouni

In receiving the Aga Khan Award for Architecture, the Palestinian Museum (*al-mathaf al-filastini*) in Birzeit reflects another stone added to the edifice of the political institutionalisation of Palestinians through culture. By institutionalisation we mean a process of regulating social facts that in turn legitimises them. Law or custom may bring this about, but, less formally, so can the standards of a professional activity. In this case, the Aga Khan Award is a cultural sector standard which, since its establishment in 1977, has seen its authority grow among architecture and museum professionals both within and outside of the Islamic world. The history of the political institutionalisation of Palestinians through culture is abundant in sectors as varied as literature, theatre, the visual arts, and cinema. This is not the place for an exhaustive account of that; the aim is rather to sketch out its main stages, using the museum as the narrative thread. This cultural model, born in its 'modern' form in Europe in the eighteenth century, soon reached the territory of Palestine. And from the first museum opened by the Ottomans in 1901 to the present day, it is even possible to distinguish three periods: the Time of Foundation Stones (1891–1967), the Time of Wall Slogans (1967–2009), the Time of the Chaotic Garden (2009 to the present), characterised respectively by nationalism, internationalism, and globalisation. The Palestinian Museum belongs fully to this last period, which has seen a proliferation of museum projects with multiple and sometimes contradictory narratives.

From Foundation Stones to Wall Slogans

The Time of Foundation Stones was the time of the first museums, and it began before the British Mandate in Palestine (1918–48), under the Ottomans. Planning for a Jerusalem branch of Istanbul's Imperial Museum (*müze-i hümayun*) dates back to 1891 and culminated in its inauguration in 1901.[1] This Imperial Museum in Jerusalem was part of an Ottoman policy of reappropriating a territory whose penetration by Europeans had extended to archaeological expeditions.[2] After their military arrival in 1917, the British took over the collection and used it as the nucleus for a Palestine Archaeological Museum. This was inaugurated in 1938 in a monumental building created for this purpose with funding from John D. Rockefeller Jr, an American citizen and son of the co-founder of Standard Oil[3] (fig. 1).

Unlike the Ottomans, the British consolidated their power not by promoting a universal imperial norm, but by encouraging local particularisms, which added impetus to the fragmentation of the empire they had helped to destroy. This dynamic, found in Iraq and in the principalities of the Persian Gulf under their protectorate, nurtured a particular current of Arab nationalism known as 'patriotism' (*wataniyya*),[4] a term that would find its way into the Arabic name of the Palestinian National (or Patriotic) Charter (*Al-Mithaq al-watani al-filastini*) that the Palestine

Figure 1. View of the Palestine Archaeological Museum, from the Mount of Olives, dated 1934

Liberation Organisation has framed. The political context of the British Mandate also enabled the opening of a Museum of Islamic Antiquities (*mathaf al-athar al-islamiyya*), or Islamic Museum, on the Esplanade of the Mosques in 1922 (fig. 2), and a Palestine Folk Museum near the Holy Sepulchre in 1936,[5] as well as museums promoting a Jewish identity, such as the Tel Aviv Museum of Art in 1932.[6] It was from a room in this museum specialising in Jewish artists from around the world that David Ben-Gurion read the Declaration of the Establishment of the State of Israel on 14 May 1948.

After the State of Israel conquered East Jerusalem in 1967, it changed the name of the Palestine Archaeological Museum to the Rockefeller Archaeological Museum, thus erasing the country's name from its main cultural institutional support. But the political institutionalisation of Palestinians through culture did not stop; it changed form. Over the next three decades, it moved from museums to cultural events. From conferences to exhibitions and festivals, the focus shifted from archaeology to contemporary visual arts. And the British Empire was replaced by new state actors with a political interest in promoting a Palestinian identity and with the financial resources to do so, starting with the oil states of the Islamic world. This was a Time of Wall Slogans.

The creation of the Palestine Museum of Contemporary Arts (*Muze-ye honarhâ-ye mo'âser-e felestin*) in Tehran is a case in point. Its name recalls that of the Tehran Museum of Contemporary Arts (*Muze-ye honarhâ-ye mo'âser-e tehrân*), inaugurated two years before the end of Mohammad Reza Pahlavi's reign, the focus of which, apart from contemporary Iranian art,

Figure 2. View of the Museum of Islamic Antiquities, on the Esplanade of the Mosques in Jerusalem, 2009

is post-war American art. Each of these two museums with such similar names reflects a political order. The Palestine Museum of Contemporary Arts opened its doors in the year 1384 of the Iranian solar calendar, corresponding to 2005–06 (figs. 3 and 4). It is housed in a central district of Tehran in a former modernist residential villa that is also the headquarters of the International Centre for Contemporary Arts from the World of Islam (*Markaz-e beyn ol-melali-ye honarhâ-ye mo'âser-e jahân-e eslâm*). It is part of the Academy of Art (*Farhangestân-e honar*), a public organisation created in the year 2000 by the Presidency of the Islamic Republic of Iran. Of all the cultural events organised by the academy in this museum, the one that received the most media coverage abroad was in response not to a particular political or cultural event in Palestine, but to the 2005 publication in Denmark of cartoons of the Prophet Muhammad. In response, the academy launched a competition that resulted in the *International Holocaust Cartoon Exhibition (namâyeshgâh-e beyn ol-melali-ye kârikâtur-e holokost)*, which was held at the Palestine Museum of Contemporary Arts from 14 August to 14 September 2006. In the guide to Iranian

Figures 3 and 4. Views of the Palestine Museum of Contemporary Arts in Tehran, 2011

museums published in 2010–11, the museum is said to have as its main mission 'the exhibition of the art of resistance and stability' (*namâyesh-e honar-e moqâvemat va pâyedâri*), two cardinal political concepts of the Islamic Republic.[7] In the same book, the corresponding line for the Tehran Museum of Contemporary Arts gives the stated mission as 'collecting paintings by contemporary artists from Iran and the world'.[8]

However, since 1980, part of an international collection of contemporary art owned by the Palestine Liberation Organization (PLO) has been kept in Tehran, although not at the Palestine Museum of Contemporary Arts. These works, around forty in all, are part of the artists' donations collected by the Plastic Arts Section (*Qism al-funun al-tashkiliyya*) of the PLO as part of the *World Plastic Art Exhibition for Palestine (al-ma'rad al-tashkili al-'âlami min ajal filastin)*, or *International Art Exhibition for Palestine,* as it was also called in English, held at the University of Beirut from 21 March to 5 April 1978, before being extended for several weeks.[9] Until the exhibition could be turned into a museum, to be named the Museum of Solidarity with Palestine, it was intended that the collection should travel and serve as a means of political communication. To this end, part of the collection was sent to Japan, and another part to Iran. The Iranian exhibition was held in 1980 at the Tehran Museum of Contemporary Arts, in a revolutionary, 'third-worldist', anti-imperialist, and pro-Palestinian Islamic Republic. The works were still there at the time of the 1982 Israeli invasion of Lebanon, and so have remained there ever since. In 2008, two independent researchers specialising in the visual arts of the Arab world, Rasha Salti and Kristine Khouri, began to retrace the history of the 1978 exhibition. Their project, between 2015 and 2018, culminated in a book and a series of documentary exhibitions, at a range of European and American museums.[10] So, through its memory shown in museums, the 1978 exhibition has once again become a part of the political institutionalisation through culture of Palestinians on an international scale.

The Time of the Chaotic Garden

In the meantime, though, the world had changed. The major upheaval was the end of the Cold War and the discrediting of Marxism with the demise of the Soviet Union. The Time of Wall Slogans, so well embodied by the 1978 exhibition and its posters, had been succeeded by the Time of the Chaotic Garden, marked by the multiplicity of museum projects. The orderly bipolarity that the Non-Aligned Movement had challenged in vain until the 1980s gave way to a multipolar landscape, transformed by the rise of what are known as emerging countries – starting with China, where the boundary between Marxism and capitalism became blurred. Another cause of the chaos was that the ruins of the French revolutionary universalism that had nourished Soviet Marxism had become overlaid by the North American paradigm of 'diversity', with the singular noun 'nation' replaced by the plural 'communities'. The 1978 exhibition had shown an international network unified around a political organisation, the PLO, and artists from all over the world converging on a 'Third World' ideological repertoire more likely to win consensus than revolutionary Marxism alone. In this ecosystem, Palestine was a rallying slogan, with 'solidarity' appearing in French on the multilingual poster announcing the exhibition. It read 'Solidarité des artistes avec la Palestine' (Artists in Solidarity with Palestine).[11]

But now, in 2023, the Palestinian museum scene boasts dozens of specialised museums, linked to universities, places of worship, archaeological sites, and memorials to fallen heroes of the liberation struggle like Yasser Arafat and Mahmoud Darwish. From among them there emerge no fewer than four museums that enjoy international visibility, even though the Palestinians still do not have a sovereign state and are still not members of the United Nations: the Palestine Archaeological Museum, which became the Rockefeller Archaeological Museum in 1967 and is located in Jerusalem; the Palestinian Museum, launched in 2012 and inaugurated in 2017 in Birzeit near Ramallah;[12] the Palestinian National Museum of Modern and Contemporary Art, with its collection housed at the Institut du monde arabe (Arab World Institute) in Paris since a partnership was signed in 2015; and the Palestine Museum US, opened in 2018 in Connecticut by a Palestinian entrepreneur from the United States.

These four museums reflect the present currents in political discourse on Palestine conducted via culture. There is the State of Israel, which has erased the word Palestine from the museum it has taken control of, and which has put its precious archaeological collection on a tourist and scientific shelf. In 2023, the museum does not even have a website. There is only a page on the Israel Museum website devoted to it, where the word Palestine is not mentioned.[13]

Then there's the Palestinian political elite, formed around the PLO. The Palestinian National Museum of Modern and Contemporary Art, its collection housed at the Institut du monde arabe in Paris, is presided over by Elias Sanbar, a writer born in Haifa in 1947, raised in Beirut, and a translator of Mahmoud Darwish. He is also a member of the Palestinian National Council (which has been a part of the PLO since 1988), a collaborator with Yasser Arafat at the time of the Oslo Accords and Palestine's Permanent Delegate to UNESCO from 2012 to 2021.[14] This museum continues the political and cultural dynamics of the 1970s. And it was the French artist Ernest Pignon-Ernest, having taken part in the 1978 exhibition, who made possible the rapid formation of its international collection. As for the Institut du monde arabe, it too is an extension of the Time of Wall Slogans. This organisation was born at the nexus of French economic interests after the 1973 oil crisis and France's 'Arab policy', forged in the 1960s under General Charles de Gaulle, when he took France out of NATO and his foreign policy brought it closer to the Non-Aligned Movement.

Finally, there's a third group of players, the Palestinians who have made their fortune in entrepreneurship and exile. This is the group behind the Palestine Museum US in Connecticut and the Palestinian Museum in Birzeit. The latter is an older project than the Palestinian National Museum of Modern and Contemporary Art, although it stems from more recent currents of thought: those of post–Cold War globalisation. The Palestinian Museum is a 'non-governmental association registered in Switzerland with a branch in Palestine'.[15] On a Palestinian scale, it embodies the now global phenomenon of the private sector's rise to prominence in political institutionalisation generally, and culture in particular, since the 1980s. It was born out of the initiative by a group of wealthy Palestinian exiles who, in 1983, set up a non-profit organisation called the Welfare Association, or Taawon.[16] Their idea of a museum for Palestine dates back to 1997, when preparations were underway for the 50th anniversary of the Nakba,[17] which led to the dispersal of many of their families.[18]

Among the association's members is Omar Al-Qattan, son of the entrepreneur 'Abd al-Muhsin Al-Qattan (b. 1929 in Jaffa, d. 2017 in London), who made his fortune in the 1960s with a construction company in Kuwait. This enabled him in 1993 to set up the A. M. Qattan Foundation in London, which became active in Palestine in 1998. His biography on his foundation's official website states that his relationship with the PLO had its ups and downs. He financed the organisation in its early days and was a member of the Palestinian National Council until he resigned in 1990 due to a disagreement related to Yasser Arafat's support for Saddam Hussein during his occupation of Kuwait.[19] From 2012 to 2017, his son Omar presided over the Palestinian Museum project, built in Birzeit next to a university that had granted 'Abd al-Muhsin Al-Qattan an honorary doctorate in 1998 when he returned to post-1948 Palestine for the first time. The A. M. Qattan Foundation has been one of the museum's main patrons.

When Omar, the son of 'Abd al-Muhsin and an entrepreneur with economic ties to Kuwait and thus at odds politically with the PLO, took over the presidency of the Palestinian Museum, it was also a Palestinian with professional ties to the Persian Gulf, Jack Persekian, who became the director of the project. In 1998, Persekian had created an art space in Jerusalem called the Al Ma'mal Foundation (from *ma'mal*, meaning 'laboratory') and from 2004 to 2011 was a leading player in the United Arab Emirates' international cultural life, first as a curator and then as the artistic director of the Sharjah Biennial.[20] He resigned in 2011, after a controversy within the Emirati national population about a work by an Algerian artist shown at the biennial that was deemed offensive to Islam.[21] He was then available in 2012 to take over direction of the Palestinian Museum, at the time still in planning. In 2015, Persekian resigned. He returned to the Arabian Peninsula, as the director of the Museum of Black Gold (*mathaf al-zahab al-aswad*) in Riyadh.

Compared with the Palestinian National Museum of Modern and Contemporary Art, the Palestinian Museum is distinguished by its younger players, born well after the Nakba, and by its position in international cultural circles that are more artistic than literary, centred more on Dubai than Paris, and more English-speaking than French-speaking, and more multicultural than universalist, but also more familiar with the organisation of cultural events in authoritarian regimes. And they are autonomous from the PLO, if not critical of it.

The Turning Point of 2009

However, the year 2009 saw a linkage between these two networks, thanks to two events: 'Palestine's first participation'[22] at the Venice Biennale and the second major exhibition of contemporary Palestinian art at the Institut du monde arabe in Paris. Palestine's participation was not a 'national pavilion' but a 'collateral event' of the 53rd edition of the Venice Biennale's

International Art Exhibition. This regulated denomination means that it is not an official action of the Venice Biennale, but that it obeys a set of specifications and is promoted by the organisation. 'Collateral Events' can be promoted only by 'non-profit public or private institutions operating directly and primarily in the field of art, with the exclusion of both central and local territorial public institutions and administrations'.[23] The institution in question is called the 'Commissioner'. In the case of Palestine in 2009, this was Nuova Icona, a non-profit cultural association registered in Italy and dedicated to promoting contemporary visual arts.[24] The organising team was made up of Vittorio Urbani, president and founder of Nuova Icona in 1993, who acted as commissioner, Salwa Mikdadi, curator, and Rana Sadik, development director.[25] A Kuwaiti-born Palestinian art historian trained at the American University of Beirut and then in the United States, Salwa Mikdadi also became the new head of the Emirates Foundation's 'arts and culture program' in Abu Dhabi in 2009, a position she held until 2012 before continuing her career at New York University Abu Dhabi.[26] As for Rana Sadik, a Palestinian resident of Kuwait trained in business administration at Boston University, she took charge of fundraising for the project in 2007.[27] At the time, she was also a member of the board of trustees of the Welfare Association, or Taawon, which would later support the Palestinian Museum project.

The catalogue for the exhibition presented in Venice had two main authors apart from Salwa Mikdadi: Jack Persekian and Adila Laïdi-Hanieh, later to become successive directors of the Palestinian Museum in Birzeit, from 2012 to 2015 and from 2018 to August 2023, respectively. This publication stands out for its sharp criticism of the Palestinian Authority and the Oslo Accords. The former is described as a bad manager,[28] while the latter is criticised for having politically excluded Palestinians in exile,[29] the very people who created the Welfare Association.

But Palestinian participation in the Venice Biennale, *Palestine c/o Venice*, also benefited from the support of actors from the Time of Wall Slogans. One of the two 'guests of honour' at the inauguration of the Palestinian collateral event in Venice was Palestine's ambassador to the European Union and former Delegate General of Palestine in France, Leïla Shahid.[30] Other patrons of the event included the Khalid Shoman Darat al Funun Foundation (*Mu'asasa khâlid shumân dâra al-funun*). This organisation, dedicated to the private arts like the Welfare Association, was founded in Amman in 1988 on the initiative of Suha Shoman, a Palestinian artist from Jordan, born in Jerusalem before 1948 and trained in law in Beirut and Paris. In Paris, where the exhibition *Palestine: La création dans tous ses états* (Palestine: The Creation in All Its States of Affairs) opened at the Institut du monde arabe in 2009, a few weeks after *Palestine c/o Venice*, Suha Shoman, president of Darat al Funun, was present. She was even one of the selected artists. But here, the funding was no longer Palestinian. It came from the foundation of the French oil company Total and, through the Institut du monde arabe, from the French state and the states of the

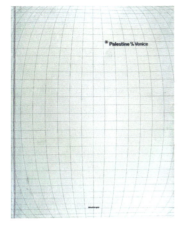

Figures 5 and 6. Cover of the catalogue for the exhibition *Palestine c/o Venice* (left) and cover of the brochure for the exhibition *Palestine: La création dans tous ses états* at the Institut du monde arabe, Paris, 2009 (right)

Arab world. The introductory text of the brochure distributed at the inauguration was signed by Mona Khazindar, in charge of collections and exhibitions at the Institut du monde arabe and co-curator of the event[31] (figs. 5 and 6). This Saudi citizen, born in the United States, educated in France, and working at the Institut du monde arabe since 1986, described the exhibition as 'an extension' of the *Contemporary Palestinian Artists* exhibition held at the Institut du monde arabe in 1997, as part of a wide-ranging programme entitled *Printemps Palestinien* (Palestinian Spring). Khazindar also associated the exhibition with 'the choice of the League of Arab States to make Jerusalem the capital of Arab culture in 2009'.[32] The evocation of the state framework was also reflected in the exhibition's title, in the form of a play on words, and on its poster (based on a work by the Palestinian artist Larissa Sansour), which showed a cosmonaut, viewed from behind, planting the Palestinian flag on the moon. Salwa Mikdadi's introductory text to the *Palestine c/o Venice* catalogue was different in this respect. 'Over the last ten years Palestinian artists have succeeded where politicians have failed', it read.[33] And the catalogue cover shows an empty planisphere.

The Palestinians still do not have a sovereign state. But they do have a museum field sufficiently well developed to make visible a string of cultural players with multiple, sometimes contradictory visions. And in this sense Palestine is not an oddity but a reflection of the contemporary world. Are not the political retreat of states before transnational or private players, their loss of sovereignty, the national fragmentation of communities economically dependent on a growing number of foreign patrons the hallmarks of our times, even in Europe? This is what we mean by the expression Chaotic Garden, which we have ventured to use in this historical sketch of the Palestinians' political institutionalisation through the museum. The garden is like Versailles without its palace, one of the earliest spectacular incarnations of the modern state. And the chaos is similar to its garden of bosquets, where, at the time of the French Revolution, each grove evoked an era in the making, over and done, or in the process of passing. To further clarify the metaphor to which the Birzeit museum in a garden lends itself, and to perhaps improve it, we would need to look more closely at artists' works, which has not been possible here. Yet it is these artists who, because of their international circulation, now give the field of Palestinian museums its unity, and whose number and quality in the global art world give Palestine another of its political singularities.

Bibliography

Primary Sources

Chakour, Djamila, and Mona Khazindar. *Palestine: La Création dans tous ses états*. Exh. cat. Arab World Institute, 23 June – 22 November 2009. Paris: Arab World Institute, n.p.

Iliffe, John Henry. 'A Folk Museum for Palestine'. *Museums Journal* 36, no. 10 (1937), pp. 420-27.

Mikdadi, Salwa, ed. *Palestine c/o Venice*. Exh. cat. Collateral Events, Venice Biennale, 7 June – 30 September 2009. Beirut: Mind the Gap, 2009.

Mojib, Jale. *Shenâse-ye muze-hâ-ye irân* [Index to the Museums of Iran]. Tehran: Parvin, 1389 [repr., 2010-11].

Perrot, Jean. 'Le Musée archéologique de Palestine à Jérusalem'. *Syria* 25, nos. 3-4 (1946-48), pp. 268-300.

Secondary Sources

Kazerouni, Alexandre. *Le miroir des cheikhs: Musée et politique dans les principautés du golfe Persique*. Paris: Presses universitaires de France, 2017.

Kazerouni, Alexandre. 'Révolution et politique de la culture à Sharjah, 1979-2009'. *Revue des mondes musulmans et de la Méditerranée* 142 (2017), pp. 165-84.

Kazerouni, Alexandre. 'Le miroir des cheikhs: Musée et patrimonialisme dans les principautés arabes du golfe Persique'. PhD thesis, 2 vols., Institut d'études politiques. Paris, 2013.

Khouri, Kristine, and Rasha Salti, eds. *Past Disquiet: Artists, International Solidarity, and Museums-in-exile*. Warsaw: Muzeum Sztuki Nowoczesnej, 2018.

Saint-Laurent, Béatrice, and Himet Taskömür. 'The Imperial Museum of Antiquities in Jerusalem, 1890-1930: An Alternative Narrative'. *Jerusalem Quarterly* 55 (2013), pp. 6-45.

Shaw, Wendy M. K. *Possessors and Possessed: Museums, Archaeology, and the Visualization of History in the Late Ottoman Empire*. Berkeley: University of California Press, 2003.

1. Béatrice Saint-Laurent and Himet Taskömür, 'The Imperial Museum of Antiquities in Jerusalem, 1890–1930: An Alternative Narrative', *Jerusalem Quarterly* 55 (2013), pp. 6–45.
2. Wendy M. K. Shaw, *Possessors and Possessed: Museums, Archaeology, and the Visualization of History in the Late Ottoman Empire* (Berkeley: University of California Press, 2003).
3. Jean Perrot, 'Le Musée archéologique de Palestine à Jérusalem', *Syria* 25, nos. 3–4 (1946–48), pp. 268–300.
4. Alexandre Kazerouni, *Le miroir des cheikhs: Musée et politique dans les principautés du golfe Persique* (Paris: Presses universitaires de France, 2017), chapter 1, esp. pp. 48–50.
5. John Henry Iliffe, 'A Folk Museum for Palestine', *Museums Journal* 36, no. 10 (1937), pp. 420–27.
6. For an official history of the Tel Aviv Museum of Art, see https://tamuseum.org.il/en.
7. Jale Mojib, *Shenâse-ye muze-hâ-ye irân* [Index to the Museums of Iran] (Tehran: Parvin, 1389 [repr., 2010–11]), p. 247.
8. Ibid., p. 246.
9. Kristine Khoury and Rasha Salti, eds., *Past Disquiet: Artists, International Solidarity, and Museums-in-exile* (Warsaw: Muzeum Sztuki Nowoczesnej, 2018), pp. 27–34.
10. The first exhibition in connection with their research took place at the Museu d'Art Contemporani de Barcelona in 2015, the second at the Haus der Kulturen der Welt in Berlin in 2016, the third at the Museo de la Solidaridad Salvador Allende in Santiago in 2018, and the fourth edition at the Sursock Museum in Beirut from 27 July to 1 October 2018. On this last exhibition, see: Benjamin Barthe, 'Beyrouth 1978, la révolution au bout du pinceau', *Le Monde*, 7 September 2018.
11. Khoury and Salti, *Past Disquiet*, p. 32.
12. Dalia Hatuqa, 'The Palestinian Museum Will Present a Culture without Borders', *The National* (Abu Dhabi), 1 June 2013.
13. On the Rockefeller Archaeological Museum, see: https://www.imj.org.il/en/wings/archaeology/rockefeller-archaeological-museum.
14. Antoine de Gaudemar, 'Elias Sanbar, intellectuel palestinien, est retourné pour les premières élections libres à Haïfa, sa ville natale, que sa famille avait fuie en 1948: Retour en Palestine', *Libération*, 30 July 1996.
15. See the history of the Palestinian Museum on its official website: https://www.palmuseum.org/en/about/the-building#ad-image-thumb-1987.
16. See Taawon's history on its official website: https://www.taawon.org/en/content/our-story.
17. The word Nakba means 'catastrophe', 'disaster,' or 'calamity' in Arabic. It has become a well-established name for the mass displacement of Palestinians and the loss and destruction of their homes and villages by the Israeli military forces in 1948.
18. See the history of the Palestinian Museum (see note 15).
19. https://qattanfoundation.org/en/about/how-it-all-began.
20. On the Sharjah Biennial, see Alexandre Kazerouni, 'Révolution et politique de la culture à Sharjah, 1979–2009', *Revue des mondes musulmans et de la Méditerranée* 142 (2017), pp. 165–84.
21. Alexandre Kazerouni, 'Le miroir des cheikhs: Musée et patrimonialisme dans les principautés arabes du golfe Persique' (PhD thesis, Paris, Institut d'études politiques, 2 vols., 2013), pp. 740 and 756.
22. Salwa Mikdadi, ed., *Palestine c/o Venice*, exh. cat. Collateral Events, Venice Biennale (Beirut: Mind the Gap, 2009), p. 5.
23. On this, see the Venice Biennale website: https://www.labiennale.org/en/art/2024/collateral-events-procedure.
24. See the Nuova Icona website: https://nuovaicona.org; see also Mikdadi, *Palestine c/o Venice*.
25. Ibid., p. 72.
26. For a biography of Salwa Mikdadi, see the Sharjah Biennial website: https://sharjahart.org/sharjah-art-foundation/people/salwa-mikdadi.
27. Mikdadi, *Palestine c/o Venice*, p. 4.
28. Adila Laïdi-Hanieh, 'Contemporary Palestinian Cultural Paradox', in Mikdadi, *Palestine c/o Venice*, p. 22.
29. Ibid., p. 23.
30. Mikdadi, *Palestine c/o Venice*, p. 4.
31. On Mona Khazindar, see Christophe Ayad, 'Une directrice générale saoudienne et atypique', *Le Monde*, 29 November 2012.
32. Djamila Chakour and Mona Khazindar, *Palestine: La Création dans tous ses états*, exh. cat. Arab World Institute, 23 June to 22 November 2009 (Paris: Arab World Institute, n.p.).
33. Mikdadi, *Palestine c/o Venice*, p. 5.

Palestinian Walks
Raja Shehadeh

It was on a spring day in 1978, the year of my return to Ramallah, that I stumbled, quite by accident, upon the legendary Harrasha of Abu Ameen, deep in the hills of Palestine.

It had been a long winter, continuing to rain throughout April and during the first few days of May, which is most unusual for this part of the world. I set out on my *sarha* just two days after the rain had stopped. The sun had emerged and the earth was not too muddy. The sky was blue with low, scattered clouds that sometimes blocked the sun, making it very pleasant to walk.

My starting point on that day was behind the Anglican School in a north-western neighbourhood of Ramallah. I walked down the newly paved road, which continued northward towards the unfinished housing development, at that time the farthest incursion of the town into the hills. I found the path almost immediately; once on it, a certain peace and tranquillity descended upon me. Now I could go on with no need to worry, just walk and enjoy the beauty of the nature around me.

I ambled alongside the western side of the valley across from the hill referred to as El Batah (the duck), so called because of the way it sits on the valley. Along the path the wildflowers were in abundance. Most were in miniature, blue irises only an inch or so high, pink flax also very close to the ground, and the slightly taller Maltese Cross and pyramid orchids, a colourful but thin carpet covering the vibrant land. I had assumed a pace that was neither hurried nor dawdling. I was heading towards the appropriately named Wadi El Wrda (the flower) across the shoulder of the hill, a gentle descent that took me over onefold, down a small incline and up another in a diagonal trajectory towards the valley.

I could see that the wadi had longer grass and plants because it was fed by the sweet water of A'yn El Lwza (the almond). I crossed over and listened to the faint sound of the dripping of the water down to a pool. Then I bent and looked into the hollow in the rocks from which the water oozed. I stretched out my hand and let the cold water run over it. There were plenty of stones and weeds. The spring was in bad need of cleaning – otherwise the water would be gushing out. I sat nearby, smelling the moist soil and looking at the impressive mossy brown cliff across the wadi. It was studded with cyclamens that grew out of every nook and cranny. They always seemed to grow in rocks that shielded them from the glare of the midday sun, squeezing themselves between cracks to prevent their bulbs from drying out. And despite their precarious position, their delicate flowers grew straight up and were hooked at the top like a shepherd's staff. Their large, variegated leaves, similar to those of the grapevines but thicker and a deeper green, seemed suspended from nowhere, miraculously hanging on the high steep rock. Above the cliff the hill was steep and from this vantage point seemed high and formidable.

Nearby I found a well-preserved *qasr*. The word, which literally means a 'castle', refers to the mainly round stone structures dotting the land where farmers kept their produce and slept on the open roof. It was in one of these structures that my grandfather Saleem and my uncle Abu Ameen camped out when they went on their *sarha* together. It must have taken a good degree of skill to build one on this slope, where it has lasted for more than a hundred years. Before visiting the *qasr*, I took a moment to look around. It was as though the earth was exploding with beauty and colour and had thrown from its bosom wonderful gifts without any human intervention. I wanted to cry out in celebration of this splendour. As I shouted 'S-A-R-H-A!' I felt I was breaking the silence of the past, a silence that had enveloped this place for a long time. My cry of greeting echoed against one hill then another and another, returning to me fainter and fainter until I felt I had somehow touched the entire landscape.

Along the terrace wall was a rock rosebush with its thick leaves and muted pink flowers. It climbed hesitantly over the stones, green against the grey as if someone had carefully chosen it to decorate this ancient wall. The stones with which the wall was built were carefully picked and piled together, and had held back the soil over many years without a single one of them falling, come rain or flood. Between these neatly arranged rocks more cyclamens grew. Their flowers stood at a 30-degree angle, pink and red droplets, all across the wall. In an opening between the two terraces were three wide stone steps placed there to make it easier to move between the two gardens. By the side of the steps was a yellow broom with its spiky green leaves. Its sweet scent filled the air. Lower down were some tall white asphodels and lower still bunches of blue sage. Even the long grass that grew along some parts of the wall added colour and texture. And when I looked up at the next level, I saw another beautiful garden, graced by a fabulous olive tree many centuries old, whose shallow roots were like thick arteries clinging together, clasping the ground firmly, forming a perfect wooden furrowed seat on which to sit and rest one's back against the trunk. Above this garden there was another. This terrace was large enough for two olive trees surrounded by a carpet of colour that spread all the way to the wall that led to yet another garden above, one garden hanging on top of another and another, going up as far as the eye could see. I felt I could sit all day next to this *qasr* and feast my eyes on this wonderful creation. What fortunate people once lived in this veritable paradise. And how wide of the mark was Herman Melville, who described this area as barren when he visited it in the middle of the nineteenth century:

> Whitish mildew pervading whole tracts of landscape – bleached-leprosy-encrustations of curses-old cheese-bones of rocks – crunched, knawed, and mumbled-mere refuse and rubbish of creation – like that laying outside of Jaffa Gate-all Judea seems to have been accumulations of this rubbish.
> – Herman Melville, *Journals of a Visit to Europe and the Levant:*
>   *October 11, 1856 – May 6, 1857*

I did not want to dwell on the vilification by Western travellers of this precious land and instead turned my mind to Abu Ameen, wondering how he managed his summers here. Was life in one of these *qasrs* so difficult that he never had time to stop and look at these gorgeous surroundings as I was doing? Perhaps he didn't need to stop to look. Perhaps his entire time in the hills with Saleem was one long *sarha* such as I might never be able to achieve.

The ponds along the wadi were filled with water from the spring. They had plenty of frogs, high spearmint, the common reed, and swaths of algae floating in the water, an unusual sight in these dry hills. This section of the wadi, called Wadi Qasrya, was wider, with the low hills on both sides seeming to recline farther and farther back. Coming down their sides were several small wadis, Wadi Shomr (fennel) and Wadi El A'rsh (the throne). I left Wadi Qasrya and began climbing the high hill to the north, with the ruin of Khirbet Sakrya, of which only a few stone houses have remained.

As I walked up, I looked at the unterraced hill to my left. What, I wondered, would it take to clear this and terrace it? What a feat it must have been to look at the wild hill and plan the subdivisions. How did they know when to build the terrace wall in a straight line, when in a curve, and when to be satisfied with a round enclave where only a single tree could be planted? They must have been very careful to follow the natural contours, memorising the whole slope before deciding how to subdivide it. The large rocks that could not be moved were kept standing where they found them. Here and there one could see clusters of them. The terracing snaked down the slope to the wadi on one side and trailed up on the other, curving with the folds of the hill, always leaving a passage for the mule-drawn hand plough to pass. Where once was a steep hill there was now a series of gradually descending terraces. In this way my ancestors reclaimed the wild, possessed and domesticated it, making it their own.

This text by Raja Shehadeh is an excerpt from the chapter 'The Pale God of the Hills' that first appeared in print in his book *Palestinian Walks* (London: Profile Books, 2007).

STONES

Palestinian Architecture and Stereotomy: Past and Present
Elias and Yousef Anastas in Conversation with Nadi Abusaada

Over the course of the last century, the architectural landscape of Palestine underwent profound transformation, ushering in a new era of urban development and expansion. Palestinian cities, some with ancient Roman origins, experienced unprecedented growth, necessitating their expansion beyond historical walls to accommodate modern needs and a burgeoning population. Key cities like Jerusalem, Jaffa, and Nablus witnessed remarkable urban expansions that introduced novel building materials, technologies, and design approaches into the region.

During this period of architectural evolution, British and Zionist colonial influence began to take root in Palestine, coinciding with the introduction of new institutions and planning regulations. Unfortunately, these changes were steered to serve colonial interests rather than the genuine needs of the local Palestinian communities. The architectural landscape became entangled with colonial ideological agendas, leading to designs that did not prioritise Palestinian society, culture, or ecological concerns.

Fast forward to today: after more than a century of Israeli settler colonialism, the architectural and construction practices in Palestine continue to bear the marks of this troubling history. Many of the architectural endeavours still serve agendas that undermine Palestinian identity and heritage.

However, amidst these challenges, a new wave of Palestinian architectural practitioners and theorists is emerging. With a keen eye on the past, they are revisiting their rich architectural heritage not merely as a nostalgic exercise but as a means to shape a future that embraces their long-rooted cultures of building and craftsmanship (fig. 1).

Figure 1. Stonemasons in Jerusalem, 1890-1900

Unlike the colonial perspective that reduces Palestinian architectural heritage to mere museum objects, these critical thinkers view it as a vibrant, living culture that holds immense potential for inspiration and innovation. By embracing their heritage, they envision a future that integrates traditional knowledge with modern sensibilities, crafting spaces that reflect the true spirit of Palestine, while addressing contemporary needs.

Through this forward-looking lens, the architectural heritage becomes a dynamic source of empowerment, reclaiming its rightful place as an essential component of Palestinian identity and collective memory. As the quest for cultural resurgence continues, Palestinian architects and theorists are paving the way for a future where architecture serves as a reflection of their resilience, creativity, and aspirations – restoring the spirit of their communities and reclaiming their rightful place on the global architectural stage.

A key example of the new architectural spirit in Palestine today is embodied by the work of Elias and Yousef Anastas. In an engaging conversation, we delve into the background and visions of these architectural practitioners, gaining valuable insights into their design and construction practices.

At the heart of this dialogue lies their experimental project 'Stone Matters', a promising endeavour that explores the enduring legacy and contemporary significance of stone construction in Palestine. As a material that has deeply influenced the architectural landscape of the country over the past century, stone holds a unique position in shaping the identity of Palestinian architecture like no other material. Through meticulous research and experimentation, Elias and Yousef Anastas shed light on the remarkable adaptability of stone construction, bridging the past with the future, and exploring its connection to global architectural history.

It is hoped that this conversation will spark a new generation of architects in Palestine and beyond who are unafraid to challenge the norms, willing to seek inspiration from their roots, and able to envision a future where architectural design becomes a transformative force for positive change. By embracing architectural experimentation, they can shape a world where buildings stand not only as physical structures but as enduring symbols of resilience, creativity, and unity.

Nadi Abusaada Please briefly introduce your architectural practice. When and how did you decide to start your practice? Where are you based? What is the geographical scope of your work?

Elias and Yousef Anastas Our practice started in 2012 when we had won a competition to build a music conservatory in Bethlehem. During construction, the budget for furniture wasn't sufficient. We decided to produce the furniture with the artisans already on site and around the city. It was the foundation of Local Industries, the design and making network part of our practice.

Figure 2. Final project result: reinforced flat stone vault in the shop of St. Mary of the Resurrection Abbey, Abu Ghosh

Since then, our practice has evolved into many shapes: industrial design, architecture, a radio station, a production-driven cultural space. We consider all of this to be an evolution of our architectural journey.

But in reality, our practice started far earlier – when, as kids, we were hanging around construction sites with our architect parents. Our practice of architecture started right there; and, in hindsight, the way we do things is sometimes similar to the spontaneity of construction sites.

Our office is based in Bethlehem. We work in Palestine but also in neighbouring countries, as well as internationally in Europe and elsewhere.

NA What are the principal interests of your architectural research and projects?

EA / YA We always focus on the buildability of our designs. It is important for us, as architects, to remain cognisant of the meaning of each project, all along the process from design to fabrication and construction (fig. 2).

Lately we have been thinking about the global idea of building less for ecological reasons. We go with a completely different leitmotif that values building as an essential primitive act. Building remains, for us, a foundational materialisation of cultural, social, and climatic practices.

Figure 3. The stone-sourcing space: a stone pavilion that adapts traditional techniques to the imperatives of resistance within the framework of the Palestinian public space

NA How does your research and practice relate to the setting you are situated in?

EA/YA We are currently writing a book of compiled material called 'Notes on Architecture in the Middle East and Elsewhere'. These compiled notes and anecdotes tell the story of peculiar ways of practising architecture in different setups, locations. What is interesting for us is the analogies in the global net of architectural practices that link and tie cultures in unforeseen ways. It is the peculiar practices of architecture that do not seem to be related in the first place, that create a global architectural solidarity standing up against a linear supremacist way of understanding the history of architecture.

This global web of solidarity is how practices coming together create theories.

NA One of your principal research areas, Stone Matters, deals with the cultural, political, and technical implications of contemporary stone construction in Palestine (figs. 3 and 4). Can you tell us a little bit about where this interest arose from? What are your thoughts on contemporary stone construction in Palestine and its treatment as a cladding material rather than a structural one?

EA/YA At first, it was a reaction to a law inherited from the British Mandate, set in 1918.[1] The law, which is still in effect today, has forced all new buildings in Jerusalem to be faced with stone. Meanwhile, the legislation has been expanded to nearly all cities in Palestine. The problem is that, while stone was favoured as a structural material, it is now only used to clad concrete structures. While this shift in the use of stone is universal, in Palestine it has taken on a particular note due to the law on stone use and the political way in which stone has been utilised to serve the interests of the occupation.

Figure 4. The pavilion becomes a symbol of innovation

Figure 5. Palestinian white stone buildings: city view of Bethlehem

In more contemporary times, although stone quarries are only present in Area C of the Palestinian territories, which is because the environmental laws in Israel are too strict to permit quarrying, they feed the entire market, including the Israeli one. The situation thus leads to an over-exploitation of the Palestinian quarries, resulting in a complete spoiling of the landscape in some areas.

Taken together, these circumstances have favoured a monotonous, unique construction technique that flattens the style of architecture (figs. 5 and 6). Our research stems from this basic situation, and from the fact that nearly all of our limestone is a hard limestone that could easily be used for structural purposes rather than just cladding – representing, in fact, a missed opportunity.

Figure 6. Palestinian quarry

NA How are you addressing this question in your own research/practice? Perhaps you could provide project examples.

EA/YA We have launched experimentation-based research into the potential for including structural stone in the language of contemporary architecture, and for combining traditional craftsmanship and materials with innovative construction techniques. Initially born of a reaction to the systematic misuse of clad stone in Palestine, the project takes its cue from the historical recurrence of stone-made architectural elements in Palestine. The architecture of Palestine combines disparate architectural elements brought by various civilisations from abroad with local elements found in situ. Through time, certain architectural attributes, originally found locally, returned to Palestine as imported architectural elements. In an attempt to blur the boundaries between local and global architecture, Stone Matters puts forward the relevance of this research beyond space and time. To this day, Stone Matters formalises into a series of site-specific, real-scale experiments (fig. 7) (a vault, a lintel, a slab, a wall) and academic articles.

Stone Matters looks at ways to drastically change how we are misusing the largest natural resource in Palestine, with the aim of placing contemporary Palestinian architecture in a more global architectural discourse.

Figure 7. Real-scale experiment by Stone Matters: a stone vault serving as a pavilion

NA What are the implications of your research/practice on the relationship between knowledge about local crafts and the introduction of new technological methods of design and construction? Could you please tell us more about your collaboration with local craftspeople and their place within your architectural design?

EA/YA Every project is a different experiment. Most of the time, projects combine advanced simulation and fabrication techniques with the local knowledge of stone masons (fig. 8). Local crafts and advanced construction techniques are inseparable. In reality, there are no experiments that can happen without craftspeople. At the same time, we are cautious about the still limited extent of the implications of our practice on crafts. In Palestine, there is more room for experimentation because industries are established by craftspeople, and as a result the implications can quickly shape industries. It is as much an opportunity as a responsibility.

In that context, our furniture design network of makers progressively evolves and takes different shapes that are linked to a production that is halfway between furniture and architecture. In a way, we are trying to build architecture with artisans. Our practice is intrinsically linked to crafts and artisanship as a way of doing things locally, as a means of creating peculiar technological simulation and fabrication techniques that are not alienated but built for a community of makers (designers, artisans, craftspeople, engineers, etc.).

Figure 8. 'While We Wait' project: a pavilion designed on a computer, cut by robots, and hand-finished by local artisans

Figure 9. AMOUD project: stone columns focusing on salvaged stone components

NA What are the main challenges that you face in exploring alternatives to the state of stone construction in Palestine, whether economic, political, or even technical? And how do you address them?

EA/YA Using stone as a structural material is a global challenge, but also an incredible opportunity. The challenges that we face and that we continue discovering are multiple.

The contemporary Palestinian city is shaped by the consumerism and short-term, profit-based economics that have prevailed globally. As a result, buildings are not meant to last beyond a couple of decades. Modern societies value the heritage of historical structures but do not look at building architecture for future heritage. In that context, sustainability is put in direct contradiction with durability. The main argument that prevails in contemporary times for not using solid materials and/or traditional techniques of construction is related to initial costs and investments, thus highlighting the lack of long-term financing of buildings. Yet, an elemental analysis of building components reveals that if the entire life cycle assessment of a material is taken into account, and provided quarries are regionally available, then solid stone construction actually is more economical than concrete. In that sense, the embodied carbon footprint of stone structures addresses an urgent global energy consumption matter, for which the building industry is more than 40 per cent responsible. In Palestine, the use of the material is even more relevant in that regard since, at any given location, the furthest quarry is just 50 kilometres away, which makes access to the material easier and its use more ecologically sound.

One of our projects, called AMOUD, focuses on salvaged stone components collected from demolished buildings in Palestine (the law is currently protecting only buildings erected before

Figure 10. Experimental vault as part of the series 'Analogy'

1917). The stone column we built addresses the issue of salvaged stone, but also the finite resource that stone quarries represent and the current political exploitation of quarries in Palestine (fig. 9). Stone quarries are mainly located in Area C (according to the Oslo Accords, Area C is a Palestinian area under Israeli security and administrative control) and serve the Palestinian, Israeli, and international market. There are no Israeli stone quarries at all because the country's environmental laws are too strict for any business to be viable, while the Palestinian stone quarries are wildly exploited. The law's existence is due to the spoiling of landscape happening a few kilometres away. Using stone in Palestinian contemporary architecture is a responsibility, as is creating a unique lexicon of architecture that ties the material to its history of techniques, while giving it a relevant position in global architectural discourse.

A sub-research area of Stone Matters is called 'Analogy' and focuses on tracing the origins of different stone structures found globally to eventually make links between forms, shapes, or techniques that are from different periods or locations and that are usually disregarded or undervalued. It helps to create a net of united practices of architectural solidarity that challenges a supremacist linear version of architectural history. It also contributes to desacralising the use of stone in architecture. In fact, the history of stone construction has been largely leaning on non-linear scientific progress (fig. 10).

The recent global interest in stone architecture, related to the aforementioned reasons including sustainability of the material, relies largely on a theory described by Robert Hooke in 1678: 'As hangs the flexible line, so but inverted will stand the rigid arch' (*ut pendet continuum flexile, sic stabit contiguum rigidum inversum*). As much as this theory is paradigmatic and allows for innovative structures in architecture, it nevertheless reduces the possibilities of stone architecture to arches and vaults, while implying that stone has no tensile strength, which contributes to the sacralisation of the material. But the study of stone architecture in a larger spectrum, from the fifth millennium BC onward, reveals that stone has also been largely and widely used for its bending capacities with trilithons, lintels, architraves, corbelled vaults, and more.

NA Do you think that the alternative methods/forms of stone construction you are presenting are scalable? I ask this especially given the expensive and labour-intensive nature of stone transport and construction, as well as the problems of affordable construction/housing in Palestine today.

EA/YA Stone Matters is an experimentation-based research project that focuses on the building of scale 1:1 elements of architecture. The scalability to architecture is intrinsic to the purpose of the research. Historically, stone construction was based on empirical principles as much as on structural principles; as such, it values labour as an essential part of its development and evolution. For instance, a wall built out of concrete necessitates double formwork, concrete, plaster from the inside and/or blockwork and plaster, paint, insulation from the inside or outside, and cladding. A wall built out of stone necessitates stone blocks. In terms of labour intensiveness, it could be argued that stone not only is less labour intensive but also relies on a transmission of knowledge that is embedded within society. Stone quarriers, for example, are incredibly knowledgeable about the geology of the mountains surrounding them. They entertain a relation to nature that is essential. They are the sommeliers of mountains. In that sense, stone is not only a material; it is a way of claiming nature, of understanding architecture, from the extraction of resources to the life of a building.

Current projects by Stone Matters include commissions for medium- and large-scale projects such as an art school in Amman, where a system of vaults, columns, and beams is being developed to be able to respond to the infrastructural needs of the different spaces (fig. 11). We are also working on making elements of architecture (including beams, columns, lintels, and slabs) available through our network of production for small and medium projects. When looking at life cycle assessment, from the moment of extraction to the erection of a building, the carbon footprint of stone remains very low in comparison with other materials. The inherited knowledge and craftsmanship around stone in Palestine make it possible to insert stone back into the common forms of architecture.

Figure 11. Model of the MMAG art school in Amman

NA Architects tend to highlight their successes. Are there any incomplete or unsuccessful projects that you would like to talk about? What did you learn from these experiences?

EA/YA In recent years we have been working on a large-scale building for a courthouse in the city of Hebron. The proposed project's shape was a direct response to the site geometry and neighbouring architectural context. Its form was responding both to the functional needs of the courthouse and to the needs of the city and the adjacent common spaces. In Palestine during the last seventy years, buildings have been planned and built around the cities in a solitary way as objects sitting on the ground and not engaging with the landscape, the city, and the urban conditions. Thus, as a result, it becomes impossible to formalise a clear vision of the territory.

    Reasons are twofold and linked both to specific political conditions and to a global state of architecture. As a result of the 1967 war, the implementation of the 1994 Oslo Accords, and the current path of the apartheid wall, there is a superimposition of pseudo borders that do not give proper limits to Palestinian cities, which are in constant threat of expropriation by the Israeli occupation. Therefore, in these areas there is a tendency to build quickly, yet without any particular objective to preserve the land.

Figures 12 and 13. View into the gallery space of the experimental education space 'Wonder Cabinet'

The Hebron courthouse is an attempt to open up the building through urban forms, and hence to encourage the public to engage with the building in different ways. The project's required programme is massive and, as such, the main architectural challenge was to embrace the size of such a building located in a rather big and urbanised city like Hebron, where there are not many similarly sized structures. Unfortunately, during the construction phase, the setup of the project – which is entirely based on international funding and implemented by highly bureaucratic institutions such as the United Nations – placed architecture and its urban implications secondary, instead putting forward agendas that seem unable to address the needs of the city and its inhabitants. Such mechanisms of dependences forged by international aid do not only affect space and time; they also tend to undermine the role and aspirations of the local agents.

NA Are you currently involved in, or plan to, extend the knowledge and expertise you are developing through your practice to the local Palestinian setting in which you operate? For example, through partnership or collaboration with local educational or cultural institutions or communities?

EA/YA Last May we inaugurated a new space in Bethlehem, the Wonder Cabinet. It encompasses our studio, production areas, a studio for artists, designers, and architects, Radio Alhara, and a restaurant run by chefs in residence. The space is meant to expand networks of knowledge and to make room for experimental collaboration among different disciplines (figs. 12 and 13). It includes a learning centre that will focus, in its first iteration, on technical professions such as welding, stone masonry, wood joinery, et cetera. For us, it signifies the foundations of an experimental education space that fosters innovative thinking through art, design, music, architecture, and gastronomy. We are also teaching a Stone Matters studio at the Columbia Graduate School of Architecture, Planning and Preservation (GSAPP) in New York.

[1] The first military governor of Jerusalem during the British Mandate, Ronald Storrs, enacted a law stipulating that all external walls of buildings should be faced with stone.

Appreciation of the Landscape:
Róisín Heneghan in Conversation with Cristina Steingräber

Cristina Steingräber Together with Shih-Fu Peng you founded heneghan peng architects in 1999, almost twenty-five years ago. Can you elaborate on how you started working together and how you became invested in designing exhibition spaces?

Róisín Heneghan We were working in New York doing competitions. A lot of competitions. We were both working with larger practices. In 1999, we submitted a portfolio to the Young Architects, a programme of the Architectural League of New York. We were selected as one of six, which gave us a little bit of momentum. We kept doing competitions, and in 2001 we won a project in Ireland. I'm from Ireland, so we decided it was going to be much easier to build a building in Ireland if we were there. So we moved, and in 2003 we won the commission for the Grand Egyptian Museum in Cairo, which was a very large project. Especially considering that only three of us were working in the office at the time. Gradually we built up, continuing to do competitions the whole time.

CS The first really large project you did as heneghan peng architects was already a museum?

RH Before that we had designed a town hall or civic office that was quite a large project. It was about 45 million euros, but the Egyptian museum was just vast in comparison. And that is really what brought us into the world of museums.

CS We are also talking about a museum today, the Palestinian Museum, which you designed after you had already completed – and I presume learned from – even larger projects such as the Egyptian museum you just mentioned. Can you please share reflections on how the Palestinian Museum's design belongs to heneghan peng architects' long trajectory of designing for exhibition spaces? What inspired you during the design process?

RH Right, I think the Palestinian Museum always has to be seen in the context of our work designing the Grand Egyptian Museum, a commission we had won without having any experience in this field. It was a very large project: the museum itself is about 100,000 square metres, the galleries are 25,000 square metres, and it is located on a site of 50 hectares. This was a huge learning curve for us. It was an open competition and we won it because we created a relationship from the galleries to the pyramids situated 2 kilometres away. We thought that there was an opportunity to have the museum with its pharaonic collection form a visual relationship.
 After winning the competition, we had an opportunity to create a design team around people we wanted to collaborate with. And one of those was West 8 in terms of the landscape.

Figure 1. Panorama view of the Palestinian landscape

When Adriaan Geuze started working on the project, he visited Egypt and also went to the Nile. One of his intuitions was that if you want to understand the story of the wealth of Egypt, you have to understand the landscape of Egypt. And how would you bring that realisation to the visitor of the museum? A lot of people go in for two hours to see Tutankhamun or some of the collection. But what we were interested in was making the visitor understand it through the landscape. The gardens of the Egyptian Museum were therefore built around trying to communicate how the landscape of Egypt formed the society. The museum gardens speak of the life of Egypt, whereas the galleries contain many funerary artefacts. We spent a lot of time at encyclopaedic museums like the British Museum or the Louvre. So, being able to step out, and having a chance to think and reflect outside, was something quite important to us.

It was this interweaving with the outside that we brought to the design of the Palestinian Museum from our experience in Egypt. The Palestinian Museum, however, is a very different kind of project. The brief was quite precise, specifying that it was difficult for people to come to the West Bank and therefore the museum was not pitched as a huge complex. Rather, it started out by being a place that can host temporary exhibitions through which the museum can develop its collection. Also, as this was a 4 hectare site, we thought that the gardens were an opportunity to create a space for visitors to look out over the landscape. One of the amazing things about the site of the Palestinian Museum is that you can see all the way to the Mediterranean. We wanted to allow the visitor to appreciate this landscape, to create a space for people to step outside and also to take advantage of the wonderful climate. This would allow the museum to host events outside expanding the range of possible activities. There were all those ideas, and, as we started to work through them, it became clear that the gardens actually were able to tell a story that would have been very hard to tell within the building (fig. 1).

CS You have spoken in the past of the concept for the Palestinian Museum emerging at the intersection of nature and culture. This can be felt in your design especially through the close relationship the museum building establishes with its surrounding garden. Can you please elaborate on how and why you chose this concept for the site in Birzeit – an undeniably culturally contested ground – and what you wanted to achieve by interlocking the two?

RH We considered many different questions, such as: How do you create a Palestinian museum? How do you bring together all the dreams, the stories, and yet leave it open enough for future generations? It is very, very loaded. Also, you are building on occupied territory. And we are Irish and Chinese-American, so we are outsiders. Who are we to say what is appropriate? But maybe you can also look at it differently: the Irish writer Samuel Beckett once said that writing in French forced him to consider every word, nothing taken for granted. As outsiders, maybe we had this benefit. In the competition stage, I was on site with some architects and one of the facility managers from the university. It was at a time when the remains of the previous agricultural terraces were still visible. Thus far everybody had been quiet, and I was the only non-Palestinian there. While taking photos I picked up some wild thyme growing in the hillside. One of the architects asked if he could take some to bring it home. And suddenly, my colleagues started talking about different dishes and became much more engaged. What was growing there clearly had given rise to all these traditional Palestinian dishes, and they were talking about different festivals involving some of these dishes. You start to realise that there was a way into the culture through the plants, and that this could be an approach to the problem of how to create a Palestinian museum. Another thing I noticed was how the stone walls in the landscape captured the water and let different plants grow in their crevices. At the time we were also reading Raja Shehadeh who had some very detailed descriptions of those walls, so it struck a chord. Actually, the site was a former hillside, so we thought that maybe we could use the motif of the wall. We started talking to Lara Zureikat, who is a landscape architect in Amman. Lara did not have the opportunity to visit the site like I did because it was very difficult for her to get into the country. But we

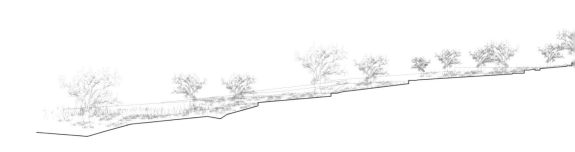

were talking about it, and I was sending her photos. She developed a concept around a landscape that moved from what she called the cultural landscape – meaning that which is currently grown in Palestine was brought into the area through its proximity to trade routes – and gradually moved to a more natural landscape. We asked ourselves how we could tell a story about the place through what had grown there. We organised the site around the landscaping contours that were already there. The walls were on site, we just picked them up a little bit. We located the museum at the top of the hill, for the view over the Mediterranean, but mostly because it was very important that it be seen. The gardens would start at the cultured terraces closest to the museum and then gradually merge with the more natural landscape at the bottom. And within that there could be, for example, the story of the citrus, the olive, the various herbs. Building up a narrative around how people live there through what can be grown there (fig. 2).

CS Lara Zureikat did the landscape, and you closely collaborated. How did this process go? And did you choose to work with her?

RH Well, when we saw the agricultural terraces and we realised that there is a lot of potential, we wanted to work with them. During the competition, we took part in a series of workshops where the jury evaluated the proposals. We had developed the idea of the terraces but had long realised that we needed to find somebody who knew the landscape. Similarly, during the Egyptian Museum project, Adriaan at West 8 had always insisted that he needed to work with somebody in Cairo who understood the region. Eventually, during one of those competition workshops, we mentioned that we needed to find somebody; they suggested some names and Lara Zureikat came up. It ended up being a perfect working relationship.

Figure 2. Cross-section of the Palestinian Museum

CS Wonderful. And I was intrigued by two references that assisted you in the conceptualising of the master plan for the hilly site. You mentioned a passage from Italo Calvino's *Invisible Cities*, and two excerpts from Raja Shehadeh's *Palestinian Walks*. Could you elaborate a little more on the role these references played in your design process for the Palestinian Museum?

RH Starting with Calvino, we have always been interested in the idea that you can understand something through a material study. By looking at what is there rather than interpreting what is there – just by looking at the city itself. With Calvino, you can tell the history of the city, for it is marked into the material fabric. You pay attention to what is there and observe carefully. And then, of course, you take your own interpretation. With Raja Shehadeh we were inspired by those beautifully observed passages about the walks in the landscape. When we came to the site of the Palestinian Museum, we started to realise that the West Bank is very, very densely occupied and every single piece of landscape has a mark on it, like the agricultural terraces we already talked about. In Ireland, for example, there is quite a lot of area without any traces of people, or very few. But in the West Bank, every single thing is touched. Shehadeh talks about how those terraces were formed, the work that went into them, and the whole world that grows within them. And so we realised that the terraces were maybe our marks in the city, if you like. And that was going to be our focus.

CS You already mentioned the stone walls of these terraces. Along the modified contour lines, they became the generator of the narrative landscape you created at the Palestinian Museum. Can you describe the choice behind the geometry and construction techniques?

RH The stone walls were already on the site, so we picked up some of them. A lot had collapsed, but we could still see the contours. At the competition stage, we proposed a contour map. Later, when we got a more accurate survey and had won the project, we refined those lines according to the actual contours. However, we made the deliberate decision to make them straight because it was not an actual farming landscape any longer. It is more deliberate, more self-conscious.

The technique we mostly used is dry stone walling. We had some higher walls as we needed to create terraces of a certain size in order to be able to get a reasonable planting area. Another consideration was that an accessible pathway through the landscape provides a wheelchair route – all of the above did result in the necessity, in some locations, of reinforced concrete walls (fig. 3).

CS I can imagine that on every construction site there might be challenges, but especially in this case, dealing with a new territory or building market you had not worked in before. We would love to hear about some of the challenges you were facing.

RH The site was handled a bit separately than the building. A lot of tasks on the site had to be done by hand. Mostly because of the nature of the site and the size of the terraces, some of the work was done with a donkey. It was a very slow process. Was it a challenge? Yes, it was. Also, they needed to find people who could actually do the dry stone walling. People had to be retrained because it is not as common anymore. Building up that expertise was a rather nice aspect of the project. But one of the things that has always struck me is how normal the project was. It followed a fairly orderly process. And of course there were some challenges, but really, compared to a lot of projects, it was a quite normal process.

CS Looking back at how you managed different skill sets and worked closely with local contractors, how did supply and labour constraints affect or modify initial assumptions or even transform the final outcome of the project?

RH The most surprising discovery for us when we started the project was that a lot of stone buildings in the area are not insulated. But we were planning a museum. For the running of the building, it is absolutely essential to have it be energy efficient. Having it insulated was very important, hence the concrete structure with stone cladding. Steel framing was needed to support the stone, which is very typical if you're building anywhere in Europe. It was not typical in this context, so we needed to work closely with the contractor. Of course, it was achievable,

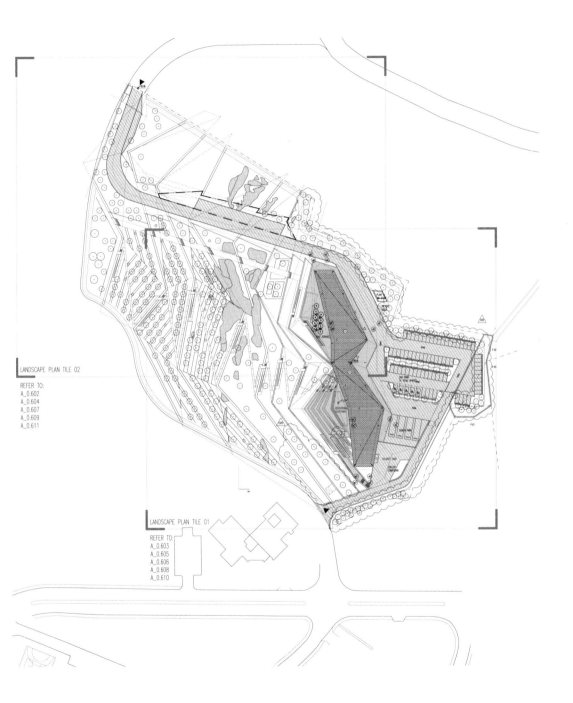

Figure 3. Site plan of the Palestinian Museum

but it was surprising to us because we did not anticipate it. Apart from that, like in any place, we needed to find out what the local skill sets are. Stonework skills are very good, and most structures are concrete, which is what we use.

CS But this is what happens with every building.

RH Yes, any place you go it is the same issue: trying to find where the skills are in this specific corner of the world.

CS You are practising architecture, landscape design, and urban design, but you often partner with other firms, such as with Lara Zureikat in this case. I would love to hear some general thoughts about this collaborative approach. When you work with other landscape designers or other urban planners, as you are doing now on your most recent project for the Storm King Art Center in New York, it seems as if you have very concrete ideas about the site and how you are going to treat it. How do you navigate other partners coming in and joining forces?

RH We are quite a small practice, with around twenty people, so we nearly always work with somebody else. And building is quite complicated. So I think in some form most people need to work with others. But we learn so much and expand our reach. For example, at the Storm King Art Center, we collaborated with WYX architecture + urban design. Storm King is an open-air sculpture park of 500 acres and, again, we try to be outside, building as little as possible. We worked with Gustafson Porter + Bowman on the landscape design and especially with Neil Porter. His reading of the landscape is extraordinary – we learned so much from him. And then Reed Hildebrand came in with a more local knowledge of the landscape, as they have done a lot of work at Storm King. So at each point something emerged that we would not have done alone. On most of our projects, we collaborate. It is always a big team, and you learn from one another. It is really important to understand that any building project is a collaborative enterprise.

CS I like that a lot. Concerning the Palestinian Museum, from your very personal perspective, what do you value most about this building and the collaborative process? What did you learn?

RH The way it is situated in the landscape is very important, in my mind. And it was not necessarily intuitive to put it where it is located today; the way it expands out into the landscape is a distinguishing characteristic. I see the Palestinian Museum as being the entire site. Not building and landscape, but the full site. To me, that is probably one of the most important things. In that project we also learned about paying more attention to looking at local skills. We really tried to observe what was possible within the guidelines that the clients wanted. They wanted to have a museum compliant with international standards, which required a certain level of performance. But we looked much more carefully at how we could realise it within the West Bank market. I will say that the client was very invested in the project; they were very well informed about construction and the museum concept. So I think that really helped the realisation of the project.

CS Did you already have a chance to go back and see it?

RH Oh, yes.

CS When you visit the site now, how does it feel to you? How are the people using the museum?

RH They have various programmes where they use the garden. I really like that. I constantly check their Twitter feed to see what is happening. What is nice is that a lot of events are held for both adults and children. I feel it is actually quite important that learning is not just about children but also reaches a more adult community. I also like the fact that they use the terraces a lot – I always love it when buildings are used in a way we had not expected.

CS That is very nice. So much is about education. Hearing you talk about it, one feels your connection to the building.

RH Yes, definitely.

Please scan the QR code to view the architectural drawings of the Palestinian Museum in detail.

Palestinian Museum, overall site plan with indication of the two access roads. The sectional profile of the access road from the south highlights the steep slope of the back portion of the site versus the gentler one of the main entrance from the north-west.

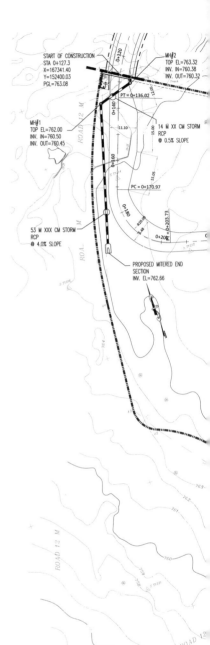

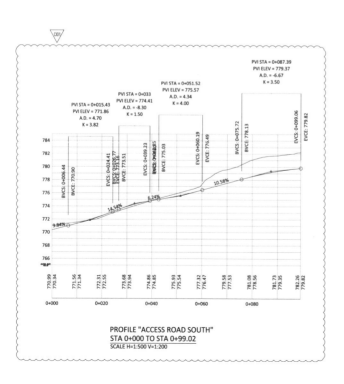

PLAN VIEW
ACCESS ROAD NORTH AND ACCESS ROAD SOUTH
SCALE 1:500

Palestinian Museum, overall plan of the storm water drainage system running in parallel with the two access roads. The simple details of the concrete gutter and drainage channel are consistent with the refined minimal feel of the built manipulation of the grounds.

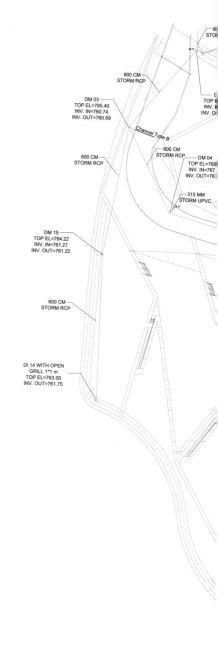

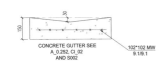

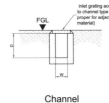

Channel Type	Depth D (mm)	Width W (mm)	Type of Channel	Type of Inlet Grating
A	100-300	300	Reinforced Concrete t=15 cm, Ø10 /20 cm	Ductile Iron or HD (Heavy Duty), Proper for load Class C250. Comply with EN1433
B	100-600	300		
C	132	98	Polypropylene	Heel Guard Ductile Iron. Slot sizes 6/95 mm, Weight Kg/m 13,5, Inlet Sectional Area 300 CM^2/M. Proper for Load Class C250. To be Comply with Standard EN 1433. Colour to be selected by the Engineer

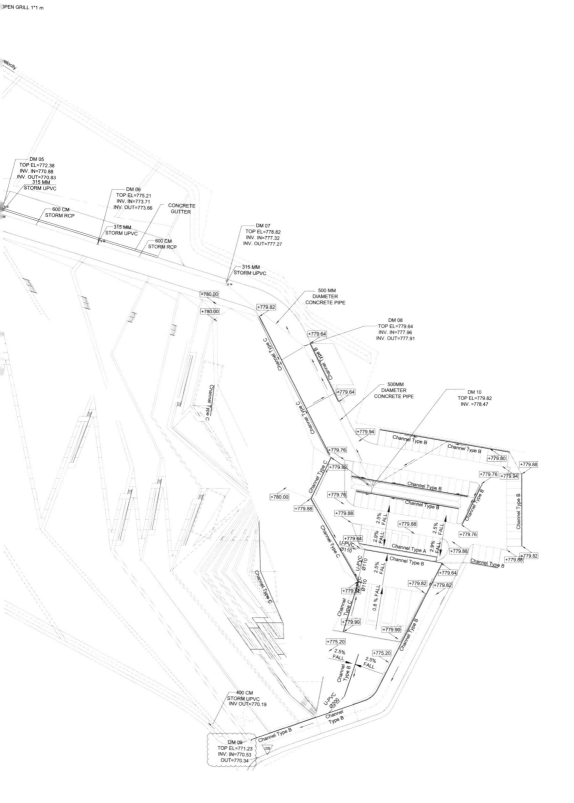

Palestinian Museum, detail of the external power plan, where the retaining walls of the terraced landscape act as primary conductors also for the lighting. It is interesting to note how moving away from the building the illumination strategy becomes progressively rarified.

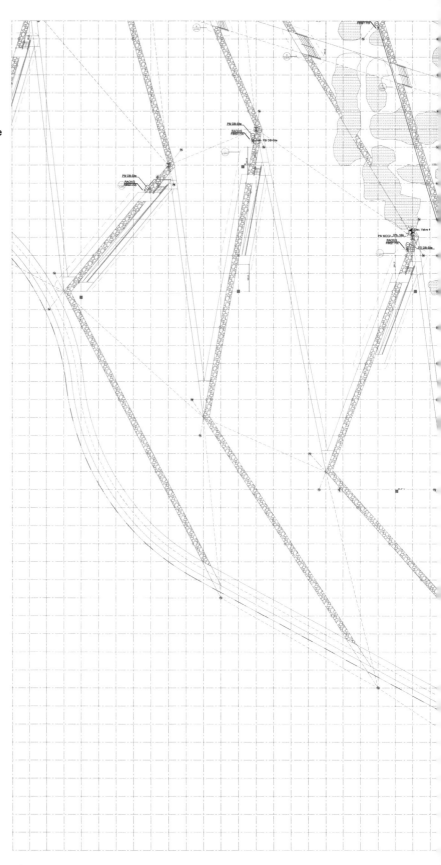

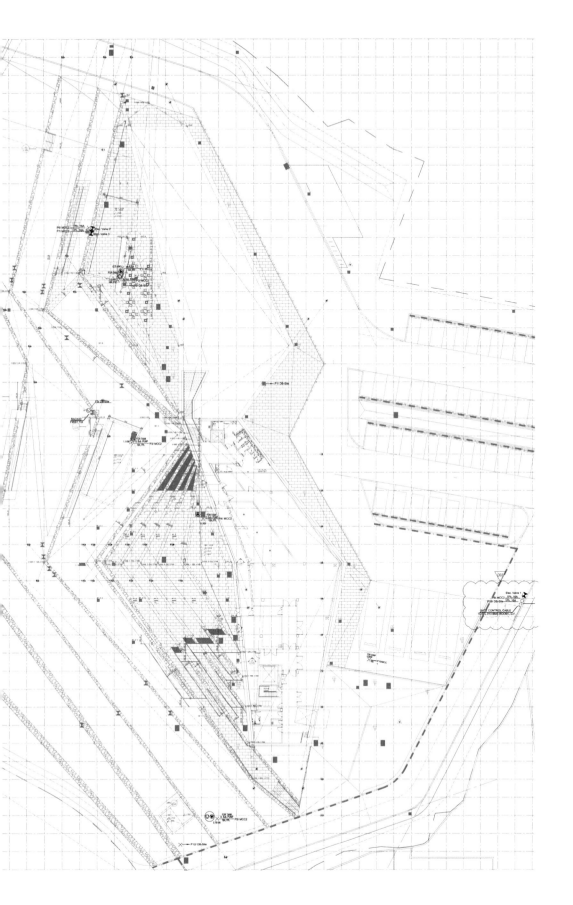

Palestinian Museum, original survey plan of the site. The topographical drawing gives us an indication of the conditions of the terrain prior to construction, and allows us to appreciate the correlation between the geometry of the retaining walls in the garden and the natural profile of the slope.

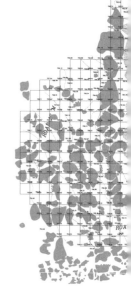

Border Coordinates		
No	Y	X
1	167334.90	152403.89
2	167437.28	152341.96
3	167455.69	152330.68
4	167452.80	152318.86
5	167450.35	152315.54
6	167455.94	152312.63
7	167463.32	152309.19
8	167470.87	152305.87
9	167472.44	152306.44
10	167479.79	152301.47
11	167486.35	152296.31
12	167492.74	152290.07
13	167496.68	152286.13
14	167500.91	152287.61
15	167509.98	152281.75
16	167516.43	152279.17
17	167507.30	152255.90
18	167571.93	152244.56
19	167571.14	152241.66
20	167567.59	152228.56
21	167540.94	152184.83
22	167534.85	152170.96
23	167532.17	152166.74
24	167527.79	152161.96
25	167524.57	152151.78
26	167521.85	152149.50
27	167518.72	152149.19
28	167517.25	152143.80
29	167516.29	152143.10
30	167514.01	152142.59
31	167511.30	152142.32
32	167507.55	152142.54
33	167499.89	152141.59
34	167494.15	152138.87
35	167490.29	152136.40
36	167477.35	152130.36
37	167470.78	152126.14
38	167465.05	152123.31
39	167438.45	152153.63
40	167364.28	152192.36
41	167337.91	152231.05
42	167309.52	152267.84
43	167303.19	152278.10
44	167307.06	152319.34

Table Of Stations			
No	Y	X	Z
S.T 853	167406.287	152219.598	771.726
S.T 1170	167543.326	152191.341	783.968
S.T 1172	167568.243	152216.081	781.433
S.T 1175	167516.233	152232.319	783.242
S.T 1176	167513.021	152267.060	782.266
S.T 1184	167499.793	152137.938	774.539
S.T 1186	167480.636	152273.658	780.410
S.T 1188	167464.609	152319.426	776.671
S.T 1190	167430.963	152338.725	773.934
S.T 1193	167417.699	152253.977	774.172
S.T 1196	167438.120	152217.009	774.601
S.T 1197	167422.382	152183.671	770.682
S.T 1198	167395.084	152217.074	770.777
S.T 1199	167378.664	152254.238	770.199
S.T 1200	167397.071	152310.044	773.576
S.T 1201	167397.058	152367.537	769.638
S.T 1202	167383.172	152341.208	771.122
S.T 1203	167356.973	152317.848	769.402
S.T 1204	167354.710	152269.751	768.141
S.T 1205	167370.296	152225.318	767.977
S.T 1206	167389.303	152184.030	767.751
S.T 1208	167358.770	152178.429	763.535
S.T 1209	167333.284	152214.875	762.485
S.T 1211	167337.153	152272.314	765.791
S.T 1212	167344.825	152327.489	767.288
S.T 1213	167384.651	152381.564	766.709
S.T 1214	167327.076	152363.342	765.327
S.T 1216	167294.699	152330.394	764.145
S.T 1221	167285.336	152211.784	758.564
S.T 1224	167281.083	152167.934	755.690
S.T 1806	167376.758	152179.521	765.249
S.T 1810	167375.237	152160.032	764.493
S.T 1871	167443.982	152153.587	770.980
S.T 1969	167463.870	152082.795	770.872

Palestinian Museum, overlay of the project above the terrain prior to execution, with indications of the boundary and fencing for the building construction site.

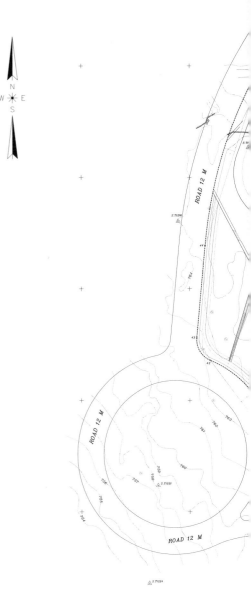

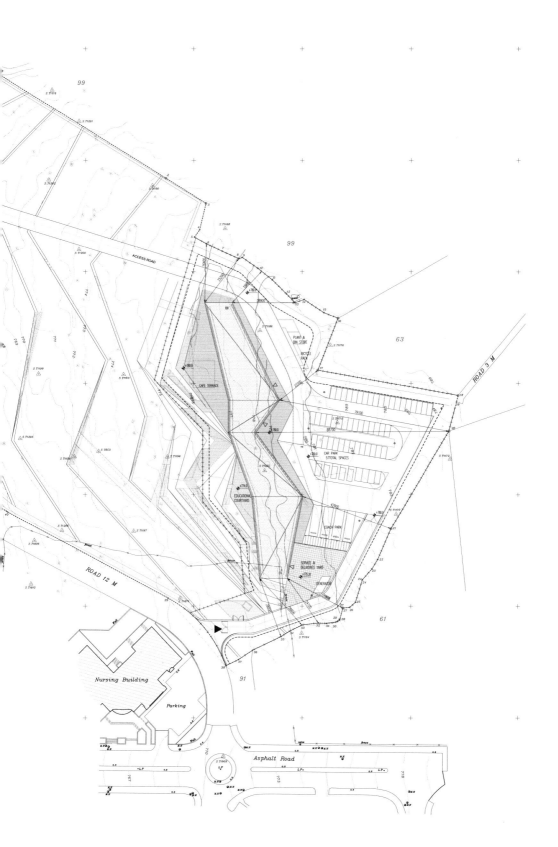

Palestinian Museum, site levelling plan for the building and adjacent parking lot at the top of the site. The different hatches describe the areas where soil was either removed or added, in order to create the base levels for the construction.

ACCESS RO

Irrigation Tank (A)

SITE BOUNDARY

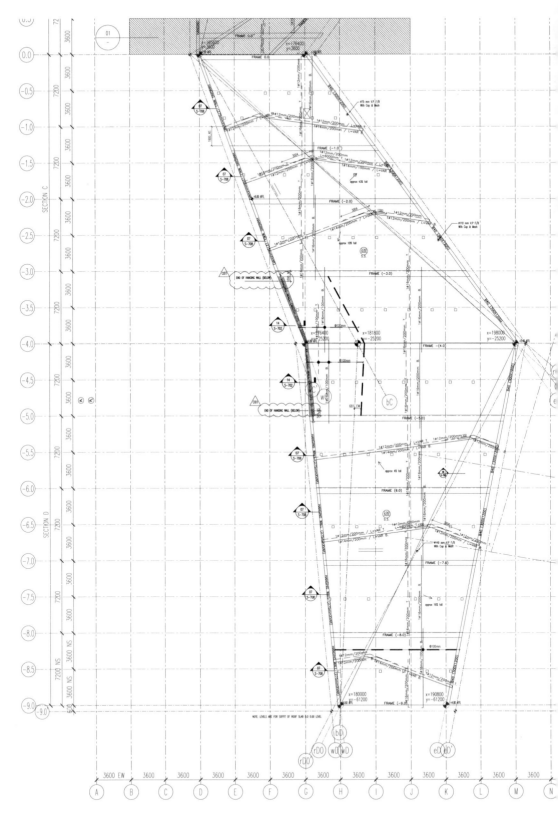

02 R.C SLAB PLAN (SOUTH) 1:100

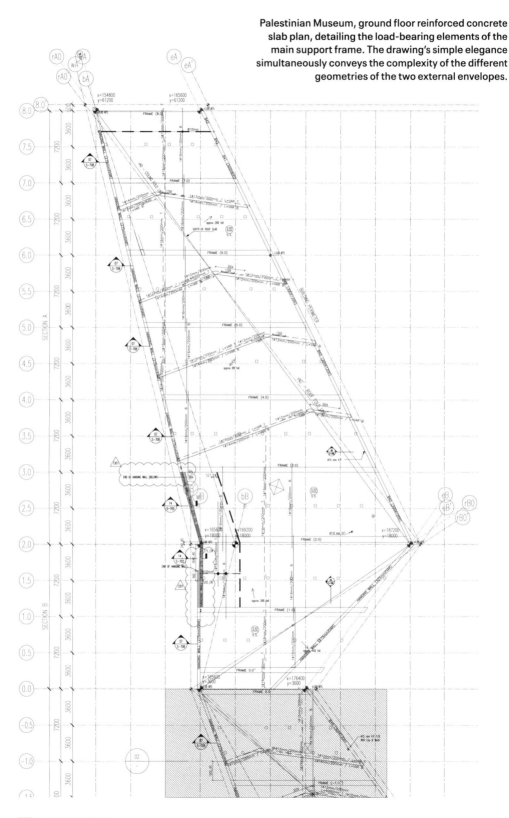

Palestinian Museum, ground floor reinforced concrete slab plan, detailing the load-bearing elements of the main support frame. The drawing's simple elegance simultaneously conveys the complexity of the different geometries of the two external envelopes.

Palestinian Museum, constructive sectional details of the stone cladding attached to the reinforced concrete load-bearing structure.
See Adrian Lahoud's piece on page 50 (esp. p. 56) for a discussion of the geometrical and technological challenge of the three-dimensional resolution of the different building envelopes.

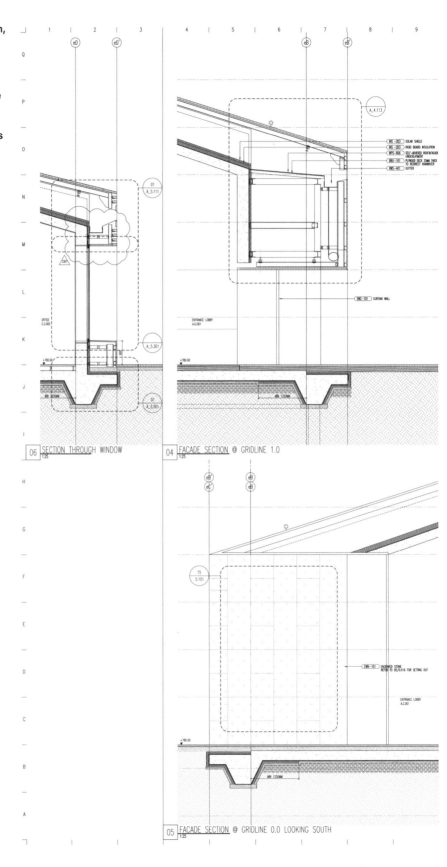

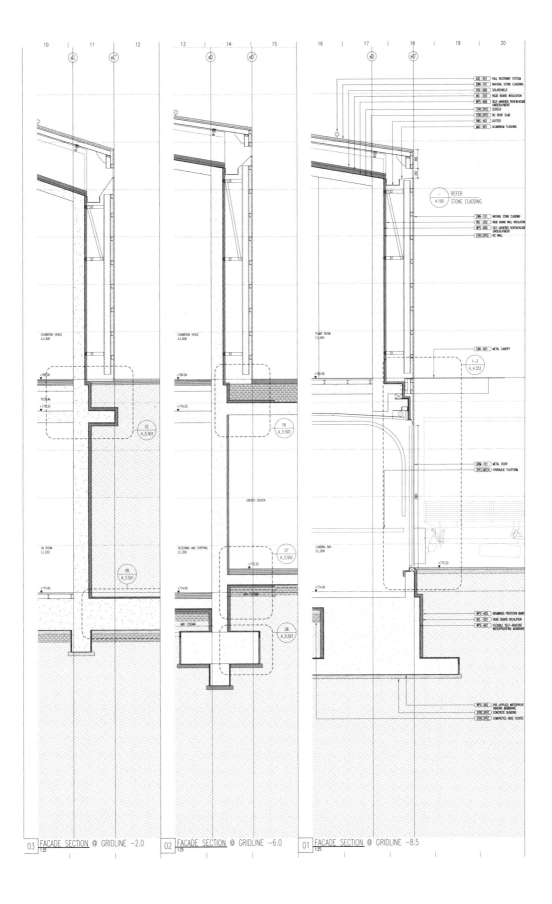

The Palestinian Museum
Hanan Toukan

How are we to think about a museum that represents a people who not only do not exist on conventional maps but who are also in the process of resisting obliteration by one of the most brutal military complexes in the world? What is, and what can be, the role of a museum in a violent colonial context compounded by the twin effects of imperialism and capitalism? Whom does the museum speak for in such a context? And what can or should it say to a transterritorial nation while physically located in a supposed state-to-be, that has no real prospect of gaining control over its land, water, or skies through current international diplomatic channels?

Three interrelated phenomena are central to thinking through these questions in relation to the Palestinian Museum located in the university town of Birzeit in the West Bank, on a hill that offers a breathtaking view of farms, terraced hillsides, and the Mediterranean Sea.[1] First, the convoluted, bureaucratic, and deceptive nature of the Oslo Peace Process and the new phase of colonisation that it inaugurated in 1993.[2] This predicament, which has been described as one of living in a 'postcolonial colony'[3] is largely defined by the paradox of living in a state without sovereignty in the West Bank and Gaza under the guise of a diplomatic process leading towards a two-state solution. Under this regime, the Palestinian National Authority (PNA), established in 1994 as an outcome of the now unpopular Oslo Peace Accords, did not gain full sovereignty for itself or the Palestinian people it 'represents'. Rather, it became the middleman of the Israeli Occupation, managing security and repressing Palestinian dissent on behalf of Israel through its own internal military and intelligence apparatus, helping to intensify Israeli colonial strategies of spatial segregation and economic control. At the same time, despite its increasing unpopularity the PNA has continued to act as the internationally recognised representative of a state-to-be in international diplomacy. This role has necessitated its participation in cultural diplomacy and top-down identity formation in an attempt to rebrand the image of Palestinians as non-violent and modern global citizens residing within the 1967 borders – processes that are key to understanding how and why the Palestinian Museum has, from its inception, had to think about representing the story of the Palestinian people outside the limits of the diplomatically sanctioned, yet now probably defunct, two-state solution.[4]

Second, one must take account of ongoing Israeli colonial practices of cultural exclusion and military domination. Supported by an architecture of bureaucratic hurdles and procedures, the Israeli occupation uses a carefully designed system of legalised, institutionalised, and normalised racial discrimination to debilitate the freedom of movement of objects, people, and ideas that a museum or any institution of knowledge production requires in order to function. As I demonstrate, the Palestinian Museum has had to and continues to manoeuvre around this in order to materialise.

Figure 1. A panoramic view of the museum's garden

Third, the Palestinian Museum has indirectly been interrogating the European museum's western-centric yet universalising mission of acquiring, conserving, and displaying aesthetic objects as part of the project of constructing nation-states and indeed modernity itself. It is precisely because of the museum's restricted spatial reality that it is able to intervene in a global discussion concerned with the role of the museum in our world. This conversation centres on the question of how to make the museum – an institution historically bound up with the emergence of the nation state and the notion of the public in eighteenth-century Europe – relevant to the global realities that shape its direction today.[5] The Palestinian Museum can be read as proposing answers to this question, first, through its mission of being 'a museum without borders',[6] and second, in the very process of its construction by drawing on the land's historically terraced-landscapes to create a structure embedded in the communities and histories it seeks to speak to and for. Through this process, the museum arguably rethinks the 'postcolonial museum'[7] as an unstable yet dynamic memory-making institution in flux, as much a living archive of violence as an affective encounter with the weight of the land and history. In doing so, it intervenes in a global conversation about the sensorial dimensions of exhibition and collecting practices in violent settings on the margins of the Global South.

Figure 2. The blank facade of the Palestinian Museum

On the surface, it is easy to dismiss the beautifully landscaped, bunker-like, low, and uneven US$24 million building that has become known as the Palestinian Museum as the vanity project of one organisation. The Welfare Association, better known by its Arabic name Taawon meaning 'cooperation', Palestine's largest humanitarian and development non-governmental organisation founded in 1983 by a group of Palestinian business and intellectual figures, has spearheaded the project in its various iterations since its inception in 1997. Headed by Omar Al-Qattan, former Chairman and acting Director of the Palestinian Museum project, board member of Taawon, chairman of the Al-Qattan Foundation,[8] and son of one of Palestine and the Arab World's most beloved businessmen and philanthropists (the late Abdel Mohsen Al-Qattan), Taawon initially played a highly visible role in the making of the museum. Taawon, which is highly regarded regionally and locally in Palestine for its financial independence, especially from western funders, and for its humanitarian work, is well known for how seriously it takes its self-proclaimed mission to 'preserve the heritage of the Palestinians, supporting their living culture and building civil society'.[9] The museum, one of Taawon's flagship projects, became a crucial site for the implementation of its heritage mandate. As with most of its humanitarian projects, Taawon relied heavily on private money donated by Palestinian business entities on the association's board such as Arab Tech Jardaneh (a private practice of consulting engineers), Consolidated Contractors Company (one of the first established Arab Construction Companies), Al-Hani Construction and Trading based in Kuwait, Projacs International (the largest Pan-Arab project management firm), as well as the Bank of Palestine.

Yet as is always the case with the building of art institutions with private sector funds, questions concerning transnational financial ties, corporate ethics, and relationships with local cultural elites were especially in the early days of the project a reminder that even the most brilliantly conceived projects encounter friction when they leave the space of conception to become transformed into concrete projects. Specifically, the process by which museums located at the nexus of the colonial/postcolonial divide reinvent their spaces and visual narrations in contexts in which the divisions between public and private are opaque, and access to landscapes and architectures necessary for the movement of objects restricted, is fundamentally a question of the political economy of cultural production. Even if the museum was able to propose innovative museum practices (which it has), its ability to survive its near impossible predicament of belonging to a 'state' that is not in a position to physically defend itself will ultimately depend on the extent to which the transnational networks, including the financial ones, that it draws upon will continue to allow it to experiment freely with different forms of knowledge production, narrations of memory, and cultural heritage preservation.

Figure 3. The Palestinian Museum's entrance area

Figure 4. A look into the pure and empty architectural space

An Empty Museum?

If there is a blotch on the museum's image that metaphorically and visually represented some of the misgivings expressed about it in its early years, it was at its official opening on 18 May 2016, when there were no art objects in the building on display. The opening took place soon after the firing of Jack Persekian, the museum's chief curator and director since 2008, and one of the Arab region's most recognised contemporary arts curators, over 'planning and management issues'.[10]

The museum was supposed to have opened with Persekian's curated project 'Never Part', which was to have featured illustrative material objects from the lives of Palestinian refugees all over the world. The 'Never Part' team envisioned and worked towards an empty museum for the opening, but they wanted interventions from artists contemplating the emptiness of the building vis-à-vis Palestine's experience of having had its material culture confiscated, destroyed, or disappeared to accompany this emptiness. The point was to reflect on Palestine's

predicament – its lack of control over borders, waters, and skies – and to question the meaning of a museum, the artefacts and collecting practices that supposedly define it, in the case of a people violently dispersed all over the globe and prevented from accessing their past and material present. Persekian and his team, conversant in global art theory and practice, were working within a genealogy of modern and contemporary art that conceptualised and theorised the museum space as an artwork and a statement in and of itself.[11]

Ironically, notwithstanding Taawon's misgivings about the curatorial conceptualisation of emptiness, the museum ended up being empty on the day of its opening thanks to a series of internal developments that culminated in the dismissal of Persekian, officially attributed to differences over 'planning and management'.[12] Despite viewing the museum as incomplete, Taawon decided to move ahead with its opening to honour the promise they had made to open it on Nakba day.[13]

It was difficult to ignore the ironies implicit in the opening of the empty museum in 2016 by the ever-unpopular Mahmoud Abbas, president of the PNA. This was especially true of mainstream Western media coverage. Headlines such as 'Palestinian Museum Opens Without Exhibits', 'The Palestinian Museum Set to Open, Empty of Art', or, more provocatively, 'Palestinian museum opening without exhibits, but creators say that's no big deal' were predictably unkind.[14] Cynically hinting at a people with neither the capacity nor the cultural history required to fill such an expensive and well-designed building, the media latched on to the fact that the museum was empty. Conveniently, these same media outlets almost entirely ignored the reality of Palestinian existence as a dispossessed people with histories, memories, and material cultures scattered all over the world or stolen by their colonisers through the cultural appropriation of music, books, art, and food, or the seizure of objects and especially archives.[15] This reality, in addition to the lack of control over the movement necessary for the travel of art objects – normally central to a museum's practice – makes compiling, acquiring, and exhibiting works an almost impossible feat.

On the Political Economy of Museums

Only a few months after the tumultuous official opening of the museum without art objects in it, in a much discussed public speech as part of the Young Artists of the Year Award (YAYA), hosted annually by the Abdel Mohsen Qattan Foundation,[16] Al-Qattan reproached the failure of the Palestinian cultural and artistic milieu in the era of Oslo to produce any meaningful dialogue or questions about the demise of the Palestinian national project.[17] Having just returned from a trip to Gaza, Al-Qattan – also the director of the Al-Qattan Foundation, one of Ramallah's most prominent cultural institutions – seemed to be lashing out at the entire cultural scene. In fact, Al-Qattan expressed the discomfort that many, if not most members of the public, including writers, intellectuals, and artists, feel in the West Bank and Gaza about the extent to which cultural work and especially the visual arts have been able to engage with the collective Palestinian experience of oppression. In his words, he wanted to use the opportunity of the YAYA to address what he described as a 'quickness, superficiality, and general disengagement with historical and political subjects'.[18]

Much has already been written about the debilitating and depoliticising effects of the NGO-isation process sponsored by international aid to the region – a process that has led to what is described by Palestinians as the collapse of the national liberation project. With globalisation and transnational cultural markets becoming the norm as elsewhere, artists and their institutions have not only been forced to readdress their role in the politics of the region and the transnational networks they need in order to survive, but also to present Palestine's plight and

Figure 5. Construction materials at the Palestinian Museum a few months before the inauguration

contributions to critical global conversations in the arts and activism more broadly. In Palestinian artist Khaled Hourani's words, 'Artists started to reconsider the perception of arts, portraits, borders, artistic values, relations of artworks and exhibits, audience and arts dealers.'[19] Whether, as a generation of artists, they were in fact able to do so without compromising on the core values of cultural resistance and the role of contemporary art in it, is today a central and uncomfortable discussion in Palestinian cultural circles.

Interestingly, on the day of the official inauguration of the museum in 2016, the building was empty of artefacts but not of objects such as the materials needed for the construction of the museum like shovels, barrels, and piles of cement. As some critics of the museum quipped, the fact that the museum was not emptied of its construction materials was a visual reminder of precisely how tied up it was in global capital circulation and real-estate development, a marker of Post-Oslo Palestine par excellence, rather than a representation of the dispossessed and oppressed people it supposedly represented.[20] This observation, which directly references the landscape dotted with cranes used to build the five-star hotels, restaurants, and upmarket housing that have come to define the 'elite-driven production of space' in Ramallah in particular, prods us to think about the tensions between the provenance of the museum's capital and what it symbolises.[21]

Landscape and Architecture

Taking up a mere 3,000 square metres of the 40,000 square metre plot on which it stands, the landscape in which the museum is set is as aesthetically and politically significant as the building and its artefacts. The visual and sensorial experience of standing in the foyer of the building is one of an affective encounter with the weight of history, the land and continued presence on it. Indeed, the topography of the land on which the museum is built, and its terraced gardens designed, were as significant to the conceptualisation of the museum as the building itself. According to Lara Zureikat, the landscape architect based in neighbouring Amman, understanding traditional practices of horticulture and working with the site's slopes and its existing plants

Figure 6. The landscape in which the Palestinian Museum is located

were central to the museum's mission to respect the cultural and natural heritage of the landscape and its determination not to disrupt it yet again.[22] This is in reference, and contrast, to the Israeli Occupation's practice of intercepting and intervening in the harmony of the landscape for settlement construction, surveillance and wall building purposes which sever Palestinians' access to cultivable land.[23] Predictably, Zureikat, who is a Jordanian national, was prevented by Israel from visiting the site of the project. She and her team resorted to the use of satellite imagery and internet communication to finalise the project. This reveals how, from the beginning, the process of turning the museum into a material reality from an idea was imbricated with the museum's objective of building on the transterritorial reality of Palestinians by thinking imaginatively about modes of delivery.

The building is therefore physically and conceptually responsive to its landscape and built environment. In the words of Conor Sreenan, chief architect of the project from the Dublin-based firm heneghan peng architects, 'It was the physical that introduced us to the geopolitical. We literally traced the existing topography and looked at the way that the landscape had been inhabited for 2,000 plus years'.[24] The idea, he explained, was not to be defined by the Occupation but rather to take back control of the landscape.

The hills of the West Bank, on which sit illegal Jewish settlements, visually embody what settler colonialism entails and the consequences it has had. Some of these include moving communities into territories acquired in war – a Zionist practice that predates the establishment of the Israeli State – in addition to settler violence against local Palestinian communities and the imposition of new demographic realities on the ground that will not only threaten the form but the very possibility of a future Palestinian State. The planting on the grounds of the museum of groves of apricot, pomegranate, mulberry, cypress, olive, walnut and fig trees, lemons and oranges, herbs like zaatar, mint, and other plants that Israel has appropriated as part of a policy of erasing the memory and identity of Palestinian people, are a step towards reclaiming what has been taken away.

But standing inside the small museum and looking out of the floor-to-ceiling windows that adorn an entire wall that overlooks the hills and the Mediterranean Sea in the distance that Palestinians are barred from reaching, thanks to Israeli imposed restrictions on movement, the foundation on which Zionism stands is usurped, even mocked, if only momentarily. In other words, instead of directly confronting politics as such, the museum may in fact be aiming to create a platform from which to expand the meaning of the political to include not only critical thought and the collection and exhibition of dispersed art, but also to link the lived and built environments and peoples' relationships to each of these. With this in mind, even the sight of the unpopular Mahmoud Abbas cutting the ribbon on the opening day becomes more palatable.

The Art Institution, the State, and Decolonisation

The PNA complained about the museum's apparent appropriation of what it saw as the state's role of cultural patronage, most visibly in the name the museum chose for itself: 'The Palestinian Museum'. Despite this point of contention, Taawon felt the need to be courteous and to invite the president because in the end, as Al-Qattan explained, 'we need to work with the existing bureaucratic structure and engage it, regardless of who is in power. We cannot function in isolation'.[25] Al-Qattan's reasoning might sit uncomfortably with activists who see resisting colonial violence as a fundamentally confrontational act that requires tackling head-on the PNA's role as middle-man of the Occupation. Yet it is perhaps the only way in which to get a grand project of this kind off the ground in colonised Palestine today. The question that this reality begs is whether a museum of this kind was needed and whether Taawon would have done better to distribute its millions to the multitude of artists, writers, film-makers, collectives, activists, and smaller-scale arts organisations that are working laboriously to collect and document Palestine's history and cultural heritage – a question I heard on numerous occasions in the field.

To appreciate what a significant institution the museum is, despite its precariousness and rocky beginning, we need to revisit Palestinian historian Beshara Doumani's original conception of the project and the strategic plan he envisioned for it. Doumani was invited by Taawon in 2010 to submit a proposal for a museum to the organisation's Palestinian Museum Task Force. To this day, the museum continues to use his original proposal as the blueprint for ongoing development of the project, even if it has been modified somewhat along the way. Doumani envisioned the museum as 'post-territorial' (in its need to encompass Palestinians who are scattered transterritorially and unable to access their homeland) and as 'a mobilising and interactive cultural project that can stitch together the fragmented Palestinian body politic by presenting a wide variety of narratives about the relationships of Palestinians to the land, to each other and to the wider world'.[26] His starting point wasn't the geographical locale of the West Bank and Gaza – even if the museum building would be situated near Ramallah, the purported capital of a future Palestinian State – but rather the dispersed and divided Palestinian population brought together through online technology.[27] This population is composed of Gazans under siege, Jerusalemite Palestinians walled off from the rest of their people, Palestinians living in the West Bank who are intercepted, harassed, enclosed, and surrounded by a complex of Israeli checkpoints, as well the Palestinian citizens of Israel and all those living as refugees in neighbouring Arab countries and as exiles in the rest of the world.

Doumani, like Soumi and others who witnessed or remember Israel's destruction of the Palestine Information Department, sees the importance of investing in the materiality of cultural

Figure 7. *Labour of Love: Embroidering Palestinian History* exhibition, 2022-23, an artistic representation of narratives and cultural artefacts being reclaimed

practices, even if they will always be under existential threat and part and parcel of global capital circuits. In reality, the multi-million-dollar investment project that is the museum can neither be defended nor easily rebuilt, should Israel decide to destroy it at any point. The museum, like other initiatives in Palestine, whether 'state'- or civil society-led, is vulnerable to the closures, looting, and destruction to which all Palestinian cultural heritage has always been subject. This destruction is a possibility that financial investors have had to contend with. Sreenan describes the stoic perseverance of financial and other investors in the project during the dark days of the Gaza slaughter by Israel in 2014 as 'possibly one of the most graceful acts of resistance one could ever witness'.[28]

Hence the question of the museum's role vis-à-vis the power structures it has to counter in the case of Israel and contend with in the case of the PNA was never one about whether its construction would in and of itself be a compromise with the post-Oslo configuration of power. Rather, it was always about how it would negotiate with these power structures in order to position itself as a space of critique, resistance, and decoloniality in the convoluted colonial context of Post-Oslo Palestine. As Doumani puts it, complicating the issue, 'How this is done, of course, is of utmost importance'.[29]

The Palestinian Museum's mission of wresting back the narratives, material culture, and memories that have been so crudely taken away from the Palestinian people is a reminder of an integral element of decolonisation. If we think of decolonisation in the realm of museum curation as entailing not simply a decentring of the art market and the flows of art sales as suggested in the decolonial claims of Walter Mignolo and others,[30] but also a forestalling of the violence of amnesia and narrative erasure that accompanies colonialism in Palestine, a new emancipatory definition of the term may be enunciated. For all its faults and the criticism it might incur in the future, the Palestinian Museum is ultimately striving to seize control over its destiny not only from its oppressor Israel but also from hegemonic understandings and practices of statehood, peoplehood, space, time, and architecture. For that, it should be celebrated not only as a triumphant moment in the cultural history of the Palestinian people, but also as a genuinely emancipatory moment in the grand project of epistemic decolonisation, for Palestinians and for other colonised peoples everywhere.

This text is an edited version of an article by Hanan Toukan that first appeared in print as 'The Palestinian Museum', *Radical Philosophy* 203 (December 2018), pp.10–22.

---

1. It is not my intention in this article to deal with the programmatic direction, thematic focus, and evolving organisational structure of the museum. Nor do I tackle the museum's early exhibitions, *Jerusalem Lives* and *Labour of Love: New Approaches to Palestinian Embroidery*, even though they are part of the larger research project from which this article stems. Here, I am interested in the conceptual underpinnings of the museum and how they relate to more general questions about the political economy of art institutions in violent and marginal contexts.

2. Adam Hanieh, 'The Oslo Illusion,' *Jacobin* (April 2013), jacobinmag.com/2013/04/the-oslo-illusion.

3. Joseph Massad, 'The "Post-colonial" Colony: Time, Space, and Bodies in Palestine/Israel', in *The Pre-occupation of Postcolonial Studies*, ed. Fawzia Afzal-Khan and Kalpana Seshadri-Crooks (Durham, NC: Duke University Press, 2000), pp. 311–46.

4. As I write these words [in 2018], Palestinians are attempting to come to terms with President Trump's declaration of Jerusalem as Israel's capital in December 2017, in effect putting an end to the two-state solution and the long-discredited Oslo Peace Process.

5. See Eilean Hooper-Greenhill, *Museums and the Interpretation of Culture* (London and New York: Routledge, 2000).

6. See the museum's website on this concept: palmuseum.org/about/the-building-2.

7. On the 'postcolonial museum', see Alessandra De Angelis, Celeste Ianniciello, Mariangela Orabona, and Iain Chambers, eds., *The Postcolonial Museum: The Arts of Memory and the Pressures of History* (Abingdon: Routledge, 2016); Sonja Mejcher-Atassi and John Pedro Schwartz, eds., *Archives, Museums and Collecting Practices in the Modern Arab World* (Abingdon: Routledge, 2016), which have paved the way for a reconceptualisation of objects and collections as 'processes or practices and not just things'; see also Elizabeth Edwards, Chris Gosden, and Ruth B. Phillips, eds., *Sensible Objects: Colonialism, Museums and Material Culture* (Oxford: Berg, 2006).

8. The A. M. Qattan Foundation (AMQF) is an independent, not-for-profit developmental organisation working in the fields of culture and education, with a particular focus on children, teachers, and young artists.

9. Taawon, taawon.org.

10 Artforum, 'Jack Persekian, Director of Palestinian Museum, resigns', 11 December 2015, artforum.com/news/jack-persekian-director-of-palestinian-museum-resigns-56674.

11 See for instance Steven Conn, *Do Museums Still Need Objects?* (Philadelphia: University of Pennsylvania Press, 2010); Edwards et al., *Sensible Objects*.

12 Artforum, 'Jack Persekian'; James Glanz and Rami Nazzal, 'Palestinian Museum Prepares to Open, Minus Exhibitions', *The New York Times*, 16 May 2016, nytimes.com/2016/05/17/world/middleeast/palestinian-museum-birzeit-west-bank.html.

13 Zina Jardaneh, chair of the board of the Palestinian Museum, interview with the author, 17 December 2017.

14 'New Palestinian museum opens without exhibits', BBC News, 18 May 2016, bbc.com/news/world-middle-east-36322756; William Booth, 'Palestinian museum opening without exhibits, but creators say that's no big deal', *The Washington Post*, 18 May 2016; 'Palestinian history museum opens without any exhibits', Associated Press, 19 May 2016, ynetnews.com/articles/0,7340,L-4805141,00.html.

15 See for instance Hannah Mermelstein, 'Overdue Books: Returning Palestine's "Abandoned Property" of 1948', *Jerusalem Quarterly* 47 (2011); Gish Amit, 'Ownerless Objects? The story of the books Palestinians left behind in 1948', *Jerusalem Quarterly* 36 (2009); Sarah Irving, '"Endangered Archives" program opens up priceless Palestinian heritage', *The Electronic Intifada*, 13 May 2014, electronicintifada.net/blogs/sarah-irving/endangered-archives-program-opens-priceless-palestinian-heritage.

16 The Young Artist Award, named after the late artist Hassan Hourani, is one of the most important events in the visual arts calendar of Palestine and has been organised on a biannual basis by the A. M. Qattan Foundation since 2000.

17 For some who were present at the YAYA ceremony, Al Qattan's words were harsh generalisations that overlooked the real achievement in getting Palestine on to the world cultural map. For others, Al-Qattan was pushing his audience to think honestly and critically about the global political economy of arts production that Palestinian artists, like artists elsewhere, have had to negotiate with, often at the expense of effacing local historical and ongoing processes of resistance. See Tarek Hamdan, 'Omar Al-Qattan: Bakae'ya Muta'akhira ... Walakin' ('Omar Al-Qattan: A Belated Jeremiad ... or Not'), *Al Akhbar*, 26 October 2016. Al-Qattan offered a detailed response to the *Al Akhbar* piece, which he saw as wrongfully representing his statement: '(Cultural) Palestine Will not Die', A. M. Qattan Foundation, qattanfoundation.org/en/qattan/media/news/omar-al-qattan-cultural-palestine-will-not-die.

18 Interview with the author, 20 December 2017.

19 Khaled Hourani, 'Globalisation Questions and Contemporary Art's Answers: Art in Palestine', in *Globalisation and Contemporary Art*, ed. Jonathan Harris (Oxford: Wiley-Blackwell, 2009), p. 301. Lara Khalidi, an independent curator from Palestine, takes up this point in her paper 'The Museum Before the Museum', presented at the Harvard Graduate School of Design, 6 November 2017.

20 Nasser Abourahme, 'The Bantustan Sublime: Reframing the Colonial in Ramallah', *City* 13, no. 4 (2009), pp. 499–509.

21 Adam Hanieh, *Capitalism and Class in the Gulf Arab States* (New York: Palgrave Macmillan, 2011).

22 Lara Zureikat, phone interview with the author, 23 November 2017.

23 Eyal Weizman, *Hollow Land: Israel's Architecture of Occupation* (London: Verso, 2012), p. 120.

24 Conor Sreenan, phone interview with the author, 5 December 2017.

25 Omar Al-Kattan, phone interview with the author, 17 December 2017.

26 Ursula Biemann, 'A Post-Territorial Museum: Interview with Beshara Doumani', *ArteEast Quarterly*, 1 February 2010, arteeast.org/quarterly/a-post-territorial-museum/?issues_season=spring&issues_year=2010.

27 I am not suggesting that this approach is the Palestinian Museum's alone. Since the late 1990s many museums have invested in an online presence by incorporating a wide range of web-based formats into their programmes and exhibits to enable access by a global public.

28 Conor Sreenan, Skype interview with the author, 5 December 2017.

29 Beshara Doumani, informal discussion with the author, Providence, Rhode Island, 4 December 2017.

30 Mignolo's understanding of decoloniality (as opposed to decolonisation) is closely linked to the process of 'delinking' as he expounds it in 'Delinking: The rhetoric of modernity, the logic of coloniality and the grammar of de-coloniality', *Cultural Studies* 21, nos. 2–3 (2007), pp. 449–514. Here he refers to a process that leads to decolonial epistemic shifts that propose alternative universalities or what he terms 'pluriversality' as a universal project (p. 453).

SEEDS

Gardens in Dialogue
Lara Zureikat in Conversation with Walter J. Hood

Figure 1. Top view of the garden of the Palestinian Museum

Gardens are powerful sources for memory. They are landscapes that are cultivated – either for sustenance, ritual, or leisure activity. They are cared for and maintained to simulate continuity, or allowed to be successional as seasons prevail. Whether vernacular or designed, the garden as an idea permeates our consciousness and has the ability to connect us to landscapes near and far. When we can project the garden from its boundary, we see a landscape transformed from a set of discrete typologies to a landscape in constant cultivation and renovation. In Christopher Thacker's *History of Gardens,* he states that gardens have many names, including grove, paradise, park, landscape, wilderness, and orchard. In this light, the garden etymology is all-encompassing, connecting us together as people.

I have lived in Southern gardens, where waxy and colourful plant names bear their origins; Northeastern gardens within woodlots and forest; and the perennial gardens of the West with their olive-green muted colour. And I have travelled around the world, where I have had moments of *déjà vu*. So when I first saw images of Lara Zureikat's Palestinian Museum garden, it was at once familiar (fig. 1)!

Walter J. Hood In my experience, creative work is never finished … changes are imminent. I have designed exhibitions and temporary installations that I never experienced first hand, which was at once liberating but also anticlimactic, yet I do not think I have ever worked on a physical project and not visited it. So, I was wondering, how do you feel about never having seen your project? How is it to make a work and never experience its manifestation?

Lara Zureikat I was fortunate enough to travel to the Palestinian Museum site and see it in person at the beginning of the design phase, but I was unable to see the finished work or even visit during the construction phase (fig. 2).

It is lucky, in a way, that creative work is never finished. Particularly in the case of this garden, because from the early stages of design, it was intended to grow with the museum as the institution develops and as collections are acquired. The garden was designed as a physical framework onto which different elements can be added throughout the life of the museum. This applies especially to the botanical collection, which was intended to be augmented over time, because many native and heirloom plants are often not readily available commercially and need to be collected and grown from seed. So, the idea was for it to evolve, to be revisited and assessed over time by the designers and the agents responsible for its inception.

Figure 2. Construction site of the Palestinian Museum

140

Figure 3. Olive harvesting in the garden of the Palestinian Museum

Although the dialogue is ongoing, not being able to see the manifestation of the work has been quite painful because the project is very meaningful to me on both a personal and a professional level. To be denied access as a result of an unjust abuse of power is a representation of the reality that Palestinians experience on a daily basis. I grew up with Palestinians who were forcibly expelled from their homeland, so I was familiar with the struggle and aware of the injustices. I had heard so many personal accounts of these injustices through family and friends. But I had never *felt* the injustice first hand until I was arbitrarily denied entry without any justification or explanation. And I recall that it was a feeling of sorrow and distress, a difficult misfortune to come to terms with.

WJH Does it give you some comfort that the project continues to evolve, and that at some point you might be able to reconnect to it?

LZ Yes, it does give me comfort and hope that I will be able to contribute to the project's evolution in a more direct manner someday, as the gardens continue to grow. And perhaps I will be able to go and see it in person. I have, nonetheless, tasted the olive oil produced from the garden so I have at least experienced one aspect of it first hand (fig. 3).

WJH The next question is something I have thought about often while writing about the American landscape and the idea of wilderness. I was raised in the Southern Baptist church tradition, and when I first travelled to the Middle East twenty-five years ago, I had a mental picture of the landscape from the Bible. When I got there, it was a much harsher landscape than I had imagined. It reminded me of being in the desert. I wondered about Judeo-Christian beliefs and mythologies around landscape. In looking at your work, I was struck by the lushness, the contrast. What are your thoughts on the idea that, within the wild landscape, landscapes do not really want to be lush, only in specific places. Could you talk a little about that?

LZ The landscape in Palestine (and Jordan) is very diverse. There are landscapes that are quite harsh and others that are relatively lush and fall in the Mediterranean climate zone. So the contrasts between lushness and harshness are ever-present (figs. 4 and 5).

Similarly, there are two types of wilderness that have influenced my approach to landscape and, consequently, the design of the museum gardens. The first is the pristine wilderness that has palpable beauty. In our region, this type of wilderness would be an oak or a pine forest. These forests are good examples of landscapes that people are drawn to and also highly value. For me, they served as inspiration to study native plant communities and also to research landscapes that are in harmony with their biogeographical region. These are the types of landscapes that we want to typically proliferate to make up for the loss of wilderness due to urbanisation and various forms of environmental degradation. And in a region where arid landscapes are dominant, they also satisfy the public's desire for a lusher landscape.

The site of the Palestinian Museum was originally an oak woodland and was transformed by terracing and by the practice of agriculture at one point in time. There were a few remnant oaks remaining on site, and so in that area we reintroduced this wilderness in the form of a native oak woodland, recalling the Palestinian natural heritage. We also planted a pine forest at the arrival zone.

While these are two typically beautiful landscapes, the oak and pine forests, there is another, or second, type of wilderness, one that is far more challenging to interpret or represent. It is the type of wilderness that dominates the hillsides in most urban areas of our region. It emerges in fallow rural lands and empty urban plots, a landscape where nature is reclaiming its domain. This landscape, which fascinated me as a child, is more subtle, its beauty not easily recognised, and it is also undervalued. Parts of this wilderness are also represented in the museum gardens. Hence, a lot of subtle, less 'charismatic' plants were combined with more adapted, 'high-performing' plants for a sense of lushness. These conditions – and, by extension, challenges – are similar in California (fig. 6).

Figure 4. Green and lush landscape: view of the oak forest near Upper Galilee

Figure 5. Dry and harsh landscape: view of the Holy Lavra of Saint Sabbas

Figure 6. Walk through the Palestinian Museum's garden

Figure 7. The Palestinian Museum's terraces provoking a dialogue with the surrounding landscape

WJH Yes, the California landscape ecology is Mediterranean. Outside of Rome, Italy, the landscape is a dull olive green. Similar to California, making landscape much more true to this ecology demonstrates that we live in a water-scarce environment. For a long time, everything here has been irrigated to the point where even the native plants need water. It is hard to find a large oak woodland, just with oak trees and no green underneath them. And in your garden, I was struck by this larger landscape that I could imagine connecting to on a more honest level.

LZ Indeed, the connection to the wider landscape is even more critical in this case due to the nature of the topography, and also to the museum's location overlooking and extending into the surrounding landscape. The idea was for the gardens to have a dialogue with this wider landscape and for it to also transform with the seasons in similar ways. So, in the drier months of summer and fall, the hillside becomes brown and yellow, and the landscape of the museum (particularly on the lower terraces) responds in a similar fashion. A very different condition from how a typical lawn would behave, which looks the same year round. In contrast, there is a dynamic variation and, as you described, a connection on a more honest level (figs. 7 and 8).

WJH That is really hard for us to do here in California. But I think what you said suggests that your work is political. Not in terms of commenting on the nation-states, but in getting people to

Figure 8. Native Palestinian scrub vegetation and plants

understand where they are, and letting them see it through the lens of the garden and the medium of landscape.

LZ That is interesting, because I hadn't considered my work to be political. I also work for a research centre, called the Center for the Study of the Built Environment (CSBE), and much of the work we do provides research support or 'fuel' for advocacy, but I was always reluctant to carry out any advocacy myself. In the case of the Palestinian Museum, your comment about getting people to understand where they are rings true, and perhaps my work is political in an indirect way. But thinking back to the early design stages, there were some more overtly political statements I wanted to make through the design of the gardens – or, as you stated, through the 'medium of landscape'. I deliberately chose to incorporate native plants with scientific names that include a reference to the land of Palestine like *Pistacia palaestina* and *Arum palaestinum* – which is, in a way, a comment on nation-states.

I also included a theme garden called the 'Garden of Perseverance' as a tribute to the perseverance of the Palestinian people. In this garden, plant species such as Mediterranean saltbush (fig. 9) (*Atriplex halimus*, which survives in extremely saline soils) and the thorny burnet (fig. 10) (*Sarcopoterium spinosum*, which has compact thorns that protect it from grazing) are a metaphor for the resilience of the Palestinian people and their ability to withstand and thrive in harsh conditions.

In this project in particular, and in contrast to other work, I felt I had the tools to make an overt political statement through the medium of landscape. The main intention was to tell the story of the Palestinian people's connection to place through this medium. To showcase native and culturally relevant plants, drystone craftsmanship, and rain-fed farming techniques speaks to the Palestinian people's intimate and generational knowledge of their land and the plants that they foraged and cultivated centuries before occupation (and still continue to cultivate today).

WJH Recently, there has been an abundance of writing and conversations around race, colonisation, and geopolitical ideas, connecting back to how we live on this planet. And in your work it appears that you understand landscape as a medium. If you begin to put together designs that

Figure 9. Mediterranean saltbush (*Atriplex halimus*)

Figure 10. Thorny burnet (*Sarcopoterium spinosum*)

allow people to see through this medium, it is as if you were composing a picture with landscapes that transports meaning. How we remember, how we experience sites. And it seems that the garden is a great vehicle for that because you have more control over the medium. Would you agree?

LZ I do agree, and it is beautifully stated. It is my aspiration to have the picture we composed with the landscape of the museum be appreciated as a form of resistance or an antidote to colonisation and cultural appropriation.

WJH Would you say that the landscape, unlike the architecture, has a way of getting people to see commonality versus difference?

LZ Yes, in more than one way. Terracing sloped sites, for example, is a technique and tradition used by many cultures all over the world (fig. 11).

WJH One of the things I am taken by is the artifice of a building versus a landscape. A building can be described and understood in a particular way, but landscapes are different in that they elude political boundaries. So to me, the idea that a landscape can cross political hurdles to make us see commonality versus difference is a powerful tool for talking about ecology.

Figure 11. The Palestinian Museum's terraces used as a gathering space

LZ Landscapes make their own boundaries – and they very often do not follow political ones. It would be interesting to see a map that juxtaposes biogeographical or ecological boundaries with political ones. Thinking about ecologies crossing political boundaries and making us see commonality is a powerful idea indeed.

WJH The landscape almost makes us look challenged in that sense.

LZ Sadly, yes! We should pay more attention to them, which reminds me of what I find fascinating about ecology in Jordan: it is the meeting point between four different ecoregions. And therefore we have very diverse landscapes meeting in a relatively small geographic location. We have African Savannah (part of the Sudanian bioregion) in the south, and in the Jordan Valley. We have Irano-Turanian steppe in the East and Mediterranean forests and shrublands on higher elevations in the north. We also have Saharo-Arabian desert landscapes. So within just a few kilometres' range we have African Acacia woodland and Southern European Aleppo Pine forests.

This diversity coexisting in harmony in one place is compelling, so we should definitely pay more attention to and learn from the landscape.

WJH Sounds like California to me.

LZ Yes, it is very similar. That is one of the main reasons I chose to study in California.

WJH Some scholars argue that landscape is a medium that we see through. That the light, ground, rocks, water, and plantings construct a picture through which meaning is projected onto a place. Would you agree? If so, how have you crafted the medium of landscape to get us to see what you want us to see?

LZ I do agree that landscape is a medium or a lens that we see through, and it shapes our understanding of a place. I would also add taste, scent, and sound to your list. Landscape is a multisensory medium that taps into memory, the subconscious, and perhaps the collective unconscious. I did think about these aspects when I was working on this landscape. I was drawing upon recollections of my grandparents' garden, remembering what was growing in it (especially the jasmine). I travelled to a lot of villages in the Palestine countryside and observed the way the terrain was shaped and transformed by its inhabitants. I was trying to identify the common threads and what was culturally relevant. What do we select from our landscape to recount a historical trajectory, and to embody familiar cultural forms, scents, and foods? What would a traditional beloved

Figure 12. Traditional beloved food *zeit wa zaatar*

Figure 13. Blue lupine (*Lupinus pilosus L.*)

food like *zeit wa zaatar* (fig. 12), which is dried oregano dipped in olive oil and eaten with bread, look like in a landscape? And how can you make legible the connection of people and their land by highlighting these aspects? One of the terraces in the gardens was planted with olive trees (for olive oil) and oregano (for the zaatar) and wheat (for the bread) in a direct reference to *zeit wa zaatar*. The gardens include other culturally relevant aromatic plants (and many of them have traditional medicinal uses) such as sage, mint, and conehead thyme. All of these plants continue to be a part of any Palestinian pantry (fig. 13).

WJH I guess for people who live in that landscape, particular memories might emerge, for example, by the smelling of herbs in the garden.

LZ Exactly, and odour-linked memories often have an emotional component, and perhaps this forges a stronger connection to or appreciation of the landscape.

WJH How would visiting your garden impact someone like me? Are there other larger connections that exist through, let's say, a larger ecology? You do not expect places across the world to be very similar, but you can really see that landscapes like California and Palestine are brothers and sisters. The inert material might be different, but the use of stone, the use of the Mediterranean flora, is so similar ...

LZ This is a very interesting question. And now that you pose it, it occurs to me that the dialogue I was having while designing the garden is a dialogue with 'ourselves' – in what I hope is the collective sense of 'us'. I didn't think about commonalities with other places or connections to the larger ecology. It was very much a dialogue about who we are, where we came from, what we value. I believe this was the focus because Palestinian culture is currently under threat. So, in a way, we want to ingrain it, and write it down, and have it be seen and recognised by future generations, and also by the world. Many people do not actually know what certain plants in culinary culture look like in the landscape, only how they look in their dish! I hope that one of the terraces in the garden dedicated to chickpeas will serve as a visual connection between hummus and its main ingredient, thus serving, along with other plants in the garden, as a connection between the physical and the culinary landscape (figs. 14 and 15).

Figure 14. Visitors taking a tour through the Palestinian Museum's garden

Figure 15. Yoga practice amid the landscape

WJH That is really beautiful and especially powerful, particularly considering the heterogeneity of different cultures and peoples. Landscape can begin to be a place of commonality, where culture is deposited through flora and materials and landscape. I do think it could be one of those things that actually finds that common ground for us to connect in.

LZ Yes, indeed. Beautifully articulated.

WJH If you had to distil it down to a simple phrase, what is one aspect you want people to see when they come to the garden?

LZ Someone once said something very simple to me when describing the gardens, and I loved the words and their significance: 'This is us.' It was the best compliment because it encapsulated what I was trying to do: to embody our culture, our natural heritage, and to have the work be recognised and acknowledged in that way.

WJH Which goes back to all the things you were just saying about memory and establishing a connection for the museum and its landscape, so it does not feel like a foreign element that just landed. When do you think you are going to see your garden?

LZ I do not know. But I am hopeful. Oppression does not last forever.

The Land Knows You, Even When You Are Lost:[1] Tuning In to Plants in Seven Acts
Mirna Bamieh

Figure 1. The Palestinian Museum hidden by the garden's dense vegetation

To cook is to listen, and sometimes it is to speak. Recipes are stories, and sometimes are storytellers. The kitchen is a space, a landscape, and a language.

This text is written in the form of acts. Seven acts, which act as if they formed a play. Each act is a scene that is marked off from the next by a recipe; think of it like a curtain, or a brief emptying of the stage. A moment to take a break, or leave the text.

The first act introduces the plants as ancestors, their power and cultural meaning. The second act moves to wild plants, claiming a space, a space under attack (fig. 1). The third act looks at the emotional challenges connected to the plant as representative – or even as a counterpart – of a communal injustice. This is further developed in act four, peaking at colonial-era agriculture. Moving to the last three acts, reflecting on the calming power of plants in situations, their place in everyday life, mostly my life. Finally, I close with fermentation as a form of wisdom, a way of becoming.

ACT I • ROOTING

In Beit Imrin, Nablus, I found myself surrounded by wild, thorny bushes of various wild zaatar varieties, reclaiming an entire hill as their home. Attempting to capture that experience in words feels inadequate, as the memory is etched in my body as a scent – a potent, enchanting aroma that permeated the hill, akin to burying your nose in the landscape's armpit and inhaling the intoxicating fragrance of zaatar (fig. 2). There you have it – an image.

On the journey back from Nablus, we were held up for hours at the checkpoint due to the political turmoil in Nablus and Gaza. In my phone's notes, I scribbled:

Inhale: the aromas of the zaatar mountains in Beit Imrin. Exhale: the brutal assassination in Gaza at dawn. Inhale: the scent of freshly smoked freekeh in Jenin. Exhale: clashes with Israeli soldiers in various areas around you. Inhale: the inspiration and visionary projects in Burqeen. Exhale: a yearning to eradicate all injustices in the world. Inhale: the assurance of a safe bed tonight. Exhale: the knowledge that more killings will occur today, tomorrow, and beyond. Words fail to convey the absurdity of occupation and the suffocating grip of colonial power.

Wild Zaatar Mix

Ingredients:

4 cups	dried zaatar (*Origanum syriacum*)
1 cup	dried zaatar (*Satureja thymra*), meant to add a stronger and more intense flavour that feels like a bite on the tongue
½ cup	toasted almonds
½ cup	toasted wild butom (*Pistacia palestina*)
½ cup	sumac spice
½ cup	toasted sesame seeds
½ cup	toasted flax seeds
2 tbsp.	olive oil
Salt to taste	

Method:

Step 1 Begin by placing the toasted almonds and butom in a food processor. Pulse them briefly, leaving some larger pieces for added texture.

Step 2 Add the dried zaatar to the food processor and mix until you achieve your desired consistency. This step allows the flavours to meld together harmoniously.

Step 3 Transfer the mixture to a bowl and drizzle the olive oil over it, gently rubbing it in to ensure that every ingredient is coated with the oil.

Figure 2. Syrian oregano zaatar (*Origanum syriacum L.*)

ACT II • PLANTS AS ANCESTORS
PLANT·CES·TOR (AKA PLANT·CES·TAR)

Plants, those ancient beings encompassing trees, shrubs, herbs, grasses, ferns, and mosses, are not just ordinary organisms. They are the very foundation of our existence, upon which our survival depends. These magnificent beings provide us with an abundance of gifts, from nourishment and oxygen to medicine, firewood, and shelter. But their significance extends far beyond their physical offerings.

Throughout centuries of intertwined existence with humans, plants have become vessels of profound knowledge. They carry within them the stories, traditions, and wisdom of our ancestors, acting as conduits for both spiritual and earthly well-being. In fact, plants can be seen as our ancestors' ancestors, the ancient beings whose presence, sacrifices, and brilliance have paved the way for human and animal life on this Earth.

Through intentional and reciprocal relationships with these diverse and multidimensional allies, humans have unlocked the secrets of their masterful healing powers and profound wisdom. These highly intelligent ancestors have guided us towards a deeper understanding of our true purpose, fostering harmony, peace, and balance with the natural order of the universe that sustains all life.

The wisdom of 'plants as ancestors' is not a mere concept, but a living practice passed down by Indigenous and traditional peoples from all corners of the globe, reminding us of the deep connection we share with these ancient beings.[2]

Oxymel (Sage, Zaatar, and Lavender)

Ingredients:

1 part   raw organic honey
2 parts raw apple cider vinegar
           (you can also make oxymels with 1 part honey, 1 part vinegar)
Mixture of unstemmed leaves and petals of sage, zaatar, and lavender
(about ¼ of the jar)

Medicinal plants of your choice. For this recipe I chose sage, zaatar, and lavender plants that I usually source from the museum's gardens (figs. 3 and 4). Together, they create a delicious and tender oxymel that calms down and supports the respiratory system and gives the body a dose of tenderness.

For an oxymel that helps in fighting colds and flus, especially at earlier stages, you can add 3–7 cloves of peeled garlic. Optional ingredients for the garlic mix: ginger, turmeric, and fresh red chili pepper.

Method:

Step 1   Fill ⅓ of the jar with honey.
Step 2   Add garlic and other ingredients of your choice.
Step 3   Pour the vinegar on top until the jar is completely full and all the ingredients are fully submerged.
Step 4   Shake the jar really well, so that the honey is completely mixed with the vinegar.
Step 5   Burp the jar to check if more vinegar needs to be added; you need your plants fully covered with the liquid mixture with 2 mm headspace from the jar's opening.
Step 6   Leave to ferment for 1 month at room temperature and take a couple of tablespoons of it whenever you feel your immunity needs support; or add it to salads for a delicious and powerful dressing.

It will keep well for many years.

Figure 3. Lavender growing in the Palestinian Museum's garden

Figure 4. Sage growing in the Palestinian Museum's garden

ACT III • BARRI, THE WILD ONES

No one gives care to the wild ones.

They don't wait to be watered, trimmed, contained within fences of care. They do not rely on human intervention or cultivation to thrive. They do not require the confines of care or curated spaces to determine their growth or protection. They follow their own path, growing and spreading as they please. They form intricate networks of support that surpass our comprehension, connecting with other organisms in ways we cannot fully grasp or dismantle.

In some languages, the term for plants translates to 'those who take care of us'.

Pickled Almonds

Ingredients:

Fresh green almonds

Aromatics: choose the aromatics you like (e.g. 1–2 garlic cloves, 1 chopped lemon, 1 tsp. black pepper berries, 1 tsp. yellow mustard seeds, some dill leaves and flowers)

For the brine: 3.5 tbsp. salt per litre of water

30 ml	raw vinegar or brine from a previous ferment
2 tbsp.	cane sugar (optional)
2 tbsp.	olive oil

Method:

Step 1 Wash the almonds well. Arrange them tightly in a jar, along with the spices and herbs of choice.

Step 2 Pour in the salty brine, making sure all the vegetables are submerged with 2 cm of brine on top, allowing for 1 cm of air space.

Step 3 Add the raw vinegar, then the oil which will help to isolate the brine from air exposure which would otherwise cause white fungus to develop on the top.

Step 4 Flip the jar over a plate and leave overnight to allow air bubbles to leave the jar, then flip it back the next day. Leave to ferment at room temperature away from direct sunlight.

The pickles can be eaten after 21 days but reach their best flavour and probiotic goodness after 4 weeks.

Step 5 Once opened, make sure you store the jar in the refrigerator to slow down the fermentation process, and to keep undesired bacteria from spoiling the ferment after air exposure.

ACT IV • LOOKING AT HISTORY

To look at the history of colonialism from a botanical perspective is to delve into its treatment of wild versus cultivated plants and its disregard for the preservation of traditional everyday wisdom.

Throughout history, colonialism has often prioritised the commercial value of plants, neglecting the ancestral knowledge of the land, its untamed flora, medicinal herbs, and seasonal rhythms. This knowledge, predominantly held and empowered by women, was dismissed and overshadowed by market-driven interests.

To look at the history of colonialism through the history of the female body and its missing accounts about experiences of women, and the omission of their contributions beyond the realm of domesticity. This includes the stories of wild women: healers, defiant wives, independent individuals who dared to live on their own terms, and those who inspired enslaved people to rise against oppression. These narratives, often overlooked, provide a deeper understanding of the multifaceted impact of colonialism on diverse communities.

Gaza-Style Dukka

Also known as 'the soil of Gazans', Gaza-style dukka is a beloved Palestinian dish that has gained popularity among the people of the region. Dukka is typically enjoyed by dipping it in olive oil, much like its counterpart, thyme.
The name 'dukka' comes from the Arabic word for 'to crush', which perfectly describes the process of making this flavourful dish. The ingredients are combined and finely crushed, with the addition of ample hot pepper to suit the Gazan palette.

Ingredients:

500 g	wheat kernels (roast until the kernels become brown and break easily)
175 g	brown lentils (you can also use a combination of 90 g brown lentils and 80 g qdamma [dried roasted chickpeas] or roasted watermelon seeds)
65 g	dill seeds
65 g	cumin seeds or 50 g ground cumin
65 g	coriander seeds or 50 g ground coriander
200 g	sumac
1 tsp.	lemon salt
300 g	roasted sesame
2 tbsp.	salt (or adjust to taste)

Red chili flakes or paprika to taste
Pistachios (optional)

Method:

Step 1   Roast all the ingredients (except for the sumac, lemon salt, and salt) in a thick-bottomed pan.

Step 2   Once the mixture has cooled down, add the remaining three ingredients and finely grind everything in a spice mixer.

Step 3   Adjust the amount of sesame, salt, and chili according to your taste preferences.

Step 4   Enjoy the Gaza-style dukka with olive oil and bread or use it as a spice mix on poultry or vegetables.

This flavourful and aromatic dish is a true representation of the rich culinary heritage of Gaza. Its unique combination of ingredients and the traditional method of preparation make it a delightful addition to any meal.

Figure 5. View of the planted terraces

Figure 6. Mediterranean saltbush (*Atriplex halimus*)

ACT V • TRACING DIZZINESS

To have your head spin, round and round, with dizziness that forms and dissolves your sense of surroundings. Everything leaks into the other; every movement gets amplified and swells.

For those who have dizziness as a malady, treading life has to be done more lightly, as our bodies have inscribed how to negotiate steps when the ground is wobbly, how to move despite destabilisation. We are able to speak despite feelings of disorientation that prevail suddenly.

For those who have dizziness as a malady, treading life has to be done more firmly, as we have gone forward when the very ground underneath us turned into mush, witnessed our bodies navigate a world marked by unpredictable change, and were able to progress when balance was lost.

There is solace to be found in the healing power of plants. It is said that for every ailment that afflicts humanity, there exists a plant that can offer relief or even a cure. And for me, that plant is saltbush (*Atriplex*), a remarkable plant with leaves that possess a salty flavour. It can be treated like a leafy vegetable, enjoyed blanched, sautéed, or used in salads, for stuffing vegetables, and with poultry (fig. 6). Its dried leaves can be added to salts or spice mixes, infusing them with a unique and medicinal quality. For me, this plant is not just a culinary delight, but a source of healing.

In the gardens of the Palestinian Museum, the saltbush grows abundantly (fig. 5). Whenever I visit the museum, I make it a point to gather a small bouquet of these leaves. Whether fresh or dried, I use them to make a soothing tea that helps calm my spinning head and restore a sense of balance.

Herbal Tea from the Palestinian Museum

You can prepare delightful and soothing herbal teas from a variety of plants with unique medicinal properties. The process of brewing herbal tea is simple and can be adjusted to suit your preferences. You can choose to use either fresh herbs or dried herbs, depending on what you have available.

To make herbal tea, start by taking a handful of fresh herbs or 1–2 tablespoons of dried herbs and adding them to 1–4 cups of hot water, which should be around 70 degrees Celsius. The amount of water you use can be adjusted based on the strength of the herb and how strong you like your tea.

Allow the herbs to steep in the hot water for anywhere from 10 minutes to several hours, or even overnight. The longer you steep the tea, the more intense the flavour and medicinal properties will be.

If you're using herbs that are sensitive to heat and you don't want to lose any of their beneficial properties, you can make sun tea. This involves steeping the herbs in room-temperature water in the sun for several hours, or even placing them in the refrigerator for several days.

Once the tea has steeped to your desired strength, strain out the herbs and enjoy your homemade herbal tea. You can drink it hot or let it cool down and enjoy it as a refreshing iced tea.

Some herbal tea mixes that I love to prepare from the Palestinian Museum's garden:
· Saltbush, lavender, and sage
· Dandelion and lavender
· Sage and zaatar
· Zaatar and lavender
· Rose and zaatar
· Buckthorn and olive leaves (fig. 7)

ACT VI • A BOUQUET OF LAVENDER FOR THE KITCHEN

I used to never understand the allure of lavender-flavoured drinks, ice cream, lemonade, syrup, or any edible item with hints of lavender. This aversion, at times bordering on repulsion, stemmed from two distinct memories that intertwined and influenced one another. The first memory dates back to my childhood, where my mother would meticulously select cleaning products with the scent of lavender. Every surface in our home was obsessively cleaned and permeated with the fragrance of lavender. This chore consumed most of my mother's time, a choice she

Figure 7. Olive leaves

made willingly. The second memory involves a man I was involved with who gifted me a lavender-scented body cream. I would diligently shower and apply the cream all over my body before going to bed. However, as the week progressed, an inexplicable repulsion towards the man began to grow within me. By the end of the week, I packed my belongings and left him. Every time I attempted to articulate the reasons to him, an overwhelming, cloying scent of lavender would steal my words away.

Years later, during one of my food research trips, I rented an Airbnb in Akka, a beautifully renovated old house. While it appeared stunning in photographs and in person, the peeling walls above my head and the suffocating smell of humidity permeating the pillows made it impossible to sleep. A friend offered me a bottle of lavender essence, suggesting I put a few drops on my pillow to aid in sleep. Miraculously, I slept deeply and peacefully. From that moment on, my love of lavender blossomed. This love extended its arms to the kitchen, and I found myself adding lavender to the herb mixes I make for my regular kombucha fermentation.

As I started producing kombucha to meet the local consumption needs of Ramallah and Jerusalem, I found myself in need of larger quantities of lavender. I sought lavender that grew in an environment free of pollution, where it could breathe fresh air and thrive alongside other carefully nurtured plants. Since 2019, I have been sending a message to Obour from the Palestinian Museum every year. She would arrange for a substantial bouquet of lavender flowers to make its way to my kitchen. I dry a portion of the lavender for decorative purposes on the dining table, make a small pillow to place in my intimate drawer, and use the rest for teas, oxymels, and kombucha production throughout the year.

Figure 8. SCOBY mushroom

Lemon Lavender Zaatar Kombucha

A delightful probiotic-rich beverage that combines the tangy flavours of lemon, the floral notes of lavender, and the earthy taste of zaatar, a perfect blend of flavours that will tantalise your taste buds.
To create this unique kombucha, you will need to go through two fermentation processes.

For the first fermentation, you will need:

2 litres	water
1 tbsp.	black tea leaves (or 1 teabag)
½ cup	sugar
1 cup	kombucha tea
1	kombucha SCOBY[3] (fig. 8)

Begin by brewing the tea in water and adding the sugar. Allow the tea to cool completely without removing the teabags. Once cooled, transfer the sweet tea to a jar and add the kombucha tea and SCOBY. Let the mixture ferment for 2-3 weeks, depending on your desired level of acidity and sweetness. Taste the kombucha periodically until it reaches your desired flavour. Once ready, bottle the plain kombucha and store it in the refrigerator.

For the second fermentation, you will need:

1 tsp.	fresh or dried zaatar (*Origanum syriacum* or any wild or farmed thyme)
1 tsp.	lavender flowers (or 2 strings of lavender flowers)
4 slices	orange with the skin
1 slice	fresh ginger (4 × 2 cm) cut into sticks (leave the peel on if you are using organic ginger)
2	raisins
1 cup	water

Brew the fresh zaatar and lavender in the water and let it cool completely. Mix the brew with the orange juice. In a flip-top bottle or two, pour ¾ of the kombucha tea and fill the remaining ¼ with the zaatar tea. Add the slices of orange and raisins. Close the bottle tightly and allow the bacteria and yeast culture to work its magic at room temperature for 2 days. Afterwards, refrigerate the kombucha for another 5 days before enjoying its fizzy goodness.

ACT VII • CULTIVATING WISDOM, BECOMING OTHERS

I am not really wise. The only wisdom that comes to me naturally is through watching time work its way on ferments. The jar, the bottle, the vessel. It turns into a space of familiarity and care in my ever-moving, ever-shifting life.

To cultivate that wisdom, I stretch my relationship to food in all directions. One direction for that stretch is towards metaphor; fermentation as a process for reflection, the way time transforms in a jar, how mothers are the true beginnings, how cultures move in waves, how freshness is a transition, how change flows, how rot is a state, how decay is not an end.

Another direction for that stretch is to devoid fermentation from metaphor, freeing it from my eyes of apathy, understanding it purely for what it is, a practice. Rejecting presumptions of human dominance, humbly understanding that it is a tangled web of relations, and we are collaborators. Realising that those cultures have proceeded us on Earth, that our survival depends on them, that without them we would not exist.

In that precarious distance – between the actual and the metaphorical – is where wisdom sprouts, and the wise steps down from the position of the teacher, the philosopher, the prophet and becomes visible at an eye level, turning into a mother, a visionary, a fighter.

You made me. I eat you. You live through me. I am your boarders. I become you. We thrive. You eat me. We transform. We become others.

Fermented Wild Zaatar

Ingredients:

2 cups	wild zaatar (while the tips of the plant work best, you can use the whole plant as well; the *Timbra capitata* or *Satureja thymra* are preferred because their thick leaves endure fermentation better)
1	chopped lemon with rind
½ tsp.	black pepper berries

For the brine:

500 ml	water
2 tbsp.	rock salt

Top the jar with 1 tbsp. olive oil

Method:

Step 1   Start by washing the zaatar leaves thoroughly. Arrange them tightly in a jar, along with the chopped lemon and peppercorns.

Step 2   In a separate bowl, mix the rock salt into the water until it is thoroughly dissolved. Pour the salty brine into the jar, making sure that all the leaves and lemon are submerged with 2 cm of brine on top, leaving 1 cm of air space.

Step 3   To help isolate the brine from air exposure, add a tablespoon of olive oil on top. This will ensure a successful fermentation process.

Step 4   Leave the jar at room temperature, away from direct sunlight, for a period of 4 weeks. The zaatar will be ready to eat after 21 days, but its flavour and probiotic goodness will reach their peak after 4 weeks.

Step 5   Once you open the jar, it is important to store it in the refrigerator to slow down the fermentation process and prevent undesired bacteria from spoiling the ferment.

You can enjoy fermented wild zaatar in salads, sandwiches, pizzas, pastas, or even paired with cheese. Its unique flavour profile and probiotic benefits make it a versatile and healthy addition to your pantry (fig. 9).

---

[1] Robin Wall Kimmerer, *Braiding Sweetgrass* (Canada: Milkweed Editions, 2013).

[2] This terminology was coined and popularised by Layla Kristy Feghali, founder of River Rose Remembrance, www.riverroseremembrance.com.

[3] SCOBY stands for 'symbiotic culture of bacteria and yeast'.

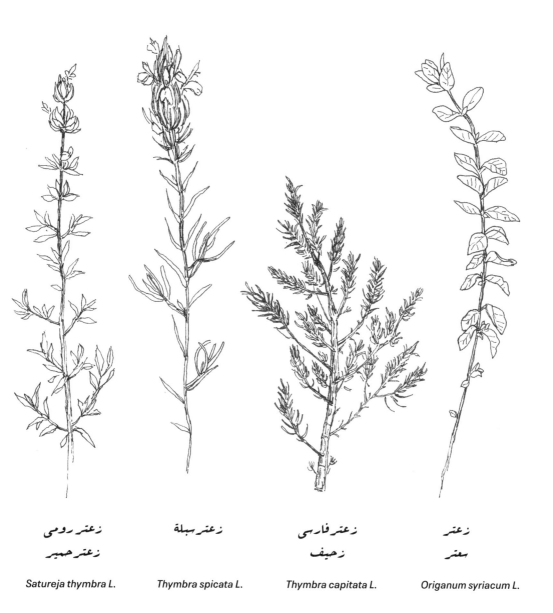

Figure 9. Yara Bamieh, illustration of different varieties of wild zaatar for printing on the napkins of the Wild Edible Plants table, dinner performance, Palestinian Museum, 2018

VOICES

ADILA LAÏDI-HANIEH

Adila Laïdi-Hanieh served as the director general of the Palestinian Museum in Birzeit from 2018 to 2023. She was the fourth director of the museum – after Beshara Doumani from 2008 to 2010, Jack Persekian from 2010 to 2016, and Mahmoud Hawari from 2016 to 2018. Laïdi-Hanieh was entrusted, for the first time after the museum opened in 2016, with developing an exhibition schedule for the upcoming years and with establishing a five-year programme strategy. Upon her appointment, she defined the museum's core mission as being to create 'emancipatory learning experiences' for the visitors, who come both from Palestine and the whole world to learn more about Palestine's rich heritage. Laïdi-Hanieh, who herself has been a scholar immersed in Palestinian art and cultural practices, as well as modern Arab intellectual history and postcolonial studies, considers the responsibility of the museum to be a producer and disseminator of knowledge about the political, economic, and social history of Palestine, using contemporary approaches.

The 'duty of care for this institution' – which exists in an occupied land and a distressed society – was formed in Laïdi-Hanieh's earlier professional life. Born in Algeria and partly raised in Jordan, Laïdi-Hanieh came to Palestine in the mid-1990s. She studied Arab studies at Georgetown University in Washington, DC, and settled in Ramallah, where she launched the Khalil Sakakini Cultural Center NGO in 1996, an institution focused on Palestinian cultural identity and support for contemporary visual arts. She acted as the centre's director until 2005 and subsequently taught at Birzeit University for two years before earning her PhD in cultural studies from George Mason University in Virginia with a thesis on the politics of contemporary Palestinian art practices. Leading up to her appointment to the Palestinian Museum, she obtained a postdoctoral fellowship from the Arab Council for the Social Sciences and published the biography of the Turkish modernist artist Fahrelnissa Zeid (1901–1991) in London in 2017 and in Istanbul in 2018.

At the museum, in tandem with developing an exhibition programme and calendar, and a five-year programme strategy, Laïdi-Hanieh started to work on developing internal institutional structures and created two new departments, one dedicated to curating, exhibitions, and collections and the other to research, education, and publications. Laïdi-Hanieh concentrated her leadership on doubling the permanent holdings of the museum, professionalising on-site and online educational programmes for chiïdren, increasing international cooperation via travelling exhibitions and heritage-protection initiatives, and supporting academic research into Palestinian culture, all with the aim to extend knowledge about Palestinian cultural heritage to a large, diverse audience. During the 2020 lockdown, all programmes were moved online, and the online presence will be further developed to also reach Palestinian families in the diaspora and in marginalised, hard-to-access areas, with the development of the first Arab museum website for children, launched in 2023 as www.sanasel.org, which brings all Palestinian Museum content and collections to a youth audience. (EN)

Adila Laïdi-Hanieh
Reflecting on the Institution

On the Significance of the Institution in Occupied Palestine
The Palestinian Museum is a non-governmental organisation established by Palestinians and funded with core Palestinian funding, principally from Taawon and its members. I found it very moving to run this institution envisioned by a prominent Taawon member, who was a friend and supporter, the formidable academic and political activist Dr Ibrahim Abu Lughod (1929-2001.) Around 1997-98, he developed the idea of a Memory Museum centred around the Nakba, and I fondly remember his passion and commitment in those years, as I was engaging with my own programmes of commemoration of the anniversaries of the 1967 Nakssa and the 1948 Nakba at the Sakakini Cultural Centre. After his passing, Taawon reconceptualised in 2010 the museum project into a forward-looking institution, with the help of Dr Doumani. After I took the helm of the museum, I redefined its mission as producing emancipatory learning experiences about Palestinian history, society, and culture. Though the political situation is not at all ideal for a museum, we chose to adopt a contemporary perspective by taking a multidisciplinary approach to producing original exhibitions, publications, conferences, lectures, and symposia, as well as websites with content for children, academics, artists, and for the general public. The institutional and physical structure of the museum allows us to leverage and gather bodies of knowledge produced about a certain topic by Palestinian artists, historians, academics, and archivists, and to present them in an immersive format bigger than the sum of its parts in original annual exhibitions, both on site and online.
Although having Palestinian funding makes our museum both independent and sustainable, we at the same time face considerable challenges and problems. In order to deal with them, we prefer to focus on the successes and the solutions that we are able to find. By deploying a variety of creative approaches involving human resolve and technology, we manage to reach the Palestinian diaspora and friends of Palestine all over the world.

On the Role of Design in Furthering the Palestinian Museum Board's Mission
The Palestinian Museum's beautiful building offers us two advantages through both its location and its intelligent design. Firstly, it reminds us of our interconnectivity as Palestinians. Living under siege and under occupation can make you forget the other components of Palestine and of the Palestinian nation. The museum's location overlooking the coast and the sea – as well as the commemoration of our donors' names around the museum and its garden, most of them from the diaspora – visually links us Palestinians living here in Palestine in the West Bank with Palestinians from the diaspora and Palestinians living on the coast. We are part of one whole – and here, at the Palestinian Museum, we are reminded of that fact every day.

View of the exhibition *Intimate Terrains: Representations of a Disappearing Landscape*, 2019

Secondly, the building represents a locally very rare, open, free horizontal built space. It is freely accessed by anyone who wishes to visit; and most importantly, it is large enough for people to roam in freely. The beautiful garden can be used by children, families, and regular visitors. Even our main exhibition hall and our lobby are wide enough for people to experience new and different ways of being in an open, unconfined space – unshackled by the utilitarian constraints of work, learning, and commerce. This truly is a spatial element very rarely found in Palestine because space is at a premium.

On the Impact of Receiving the Aga Khan Award for Architecture
Winning the Aga Khan Award for Architecture has been such a boost. First of all, it is a validation of the original dream of the founders and donors, who so long ago aimed to build a museum on the land of Palestine under occupation. More than that, though, it is an encouragement for us to continue to strive towards excellence and increase our profile internationally among like-minded institutions. The Aga Khan Award is a badge of quality, so we are humbled and honoured to have won it.

MEISA BATAYNEH

Meisa Batayneh, founder and principal architect of maisam – architects and engineers, was part of the Aga Khan Award for Architecture's Master Jury for the 14th cycle that selected the Palestinian Museum as one of six awardees. Meisa established her architecture office in Amman, Jordan, and Abu Dhabi in 1986 and has since realised large-scale international and regional construction projects in the United States, Pakistan, Cyprus, Saudi Arabia, Egypt, and the United Arab Emirates. The opportunity to serve on the Master Jury of the Aga Khan Award, and subsequently on the Steering Committee for the 2020-22 cycle, alongside colleagues such as David Chipperfield, Sarah M. Whiting, Nasser Rabbat, and Marina Tabassum, allowed Meisa to bring her expertise and local knowledge to the conversation.

Since 1980, the Aga Khan Award for Architecture has been given to building projects in triennial cycles, with each cycle being characterised by specific themes suggested to the Master Jury by a Steering Committee. The 14th cycle's themes centred, among others, around how architecture can conduct itself with respect to the economic and social changes in the Islamic world, and how it positions itself with regard to the increasing questions connected to migrations triggered by armed conflicts or environmental crises, of which the Palestinian Museum is a paradigmatic example. To guarantee independent decisions of the Award's jury, project nominators stay anonymous, and any involvement of members of either the Master Jury or the Steering Committee in nominated projects renders them ineligible. Shortlisted buildings are visited by expert reviewers who thoroughly investigate, interview, and document the projects' impact, before reporting back to the jury in individual presentations. No other award has developed such a complex and in-depth process supported by expertise to detect actual positive effects. (EN)

Meisa Batayneh

Reflecting on the Aga Khan Award for Architecture for the Palestinian Museum

On the Decision to Acknowledge the Palestinian Museum
The Palestinian Museum impressed the Master Jury: the design strength of both the building and the landscape caught our attention, and the harmony that the land and the architecture create is very evident. The building itself sits with great dignity on top of a hill overlooking the distant sea and the inaccessible historic cities of Palestine. The building radiates elegance, and its geometry blends with the landscape as if one were feeding into the other. In Arabic, we call the walls that hold the whole landscape of that area *sanasel*. And you feel like the building almost emerged out of these *sanasels*. One of the most impactful moments for us as a jury was when the reviewer who had been entrusted to visit the site and the project came back with his report. The way he described the challenges the project faced was very touching. He was elaborating on how the challenges did not stop the designers from seeking perfection in every way, on the use of materials, the way they laid the stone, the craftsmanship, and the detailing of the project. What this revelation instilled and proved to the Master Jury: not only does the project fit the criteria of design excellence, but it also creates a platform that captures the story of Palestine and the people of Palestine. It evokes emotions. It highlights the resilience and the hopes and aspirations of the Palestinian people. In that sense, the Palestinian Museum exemplifies the mission statement of the Aga Khan Award in improving the environmental, social, and cultural aspects and enhancing the quality of life through architecture. The Palestinian Museum ticks all three boxes, but I would like to specifically highlight how the museum creates a thriving hub. Locating the museum next to Birzeit University was a very strategic decision that I think made all the difference. The students have access to the museum almost like an extension of the campus, and in turn, they give life to the place. The museum holds many events, and it has an open-door policy that brings in the community through both the indoor and outdoor spaces. This takes the museum beyond it being a building that exhibits the story of Palestine to also engage the people in conversations and learning and collaboration.

On the Symbolic Value of the Palestinian Museum
The symbolic value of the Palestinian Museum is profound and multilayered. It serves as a beacon of the resilience of the people of Palestine, and the empowerment of the younger generation today and tomorrow. More than that, it embodies not only this resilience but also the enduring spirit of the Palestinian people. When I visited the museum and its grounds, it brought back a nostalgic memory of my maternal grandfather, who used to take us to his farms. What is so profound for me is that this

museum is very much like the people of Palestine. It is grounded. It is rooted. But at the same time it is modern, flexible, bold, and strong in nature. It is evident that the team spirit in which the museum was built – especially between the architect and the landscape architect – is what created the beauty that we see. As a result, the museum sends out a message to the world, inviting Palestinians from wherever they are to come and participate in creating the narrative of the aspirations and hopes of Palestine, and in emphasising the importance of preserving Palestinian culture and heritage.

On the Effect of Winning the Aga Khan Award for Architecture
As always, the Aga Khan Award for Architecture highlights projects that impact people's lives for the better. What is more important than shedding light on the suffering and hardship of the Palestinians who chose to create a museum that will express their voice and amplify it to the world? By recognising the project, the Aga Khan Award has given the Palestinian people another platform to tell their story and share it with the world. Also, when the Award validates the excellence of design of both the building or the landscape, it carries with it many values that other projects can learn from. It gives a sense of pride to have successfully erected a museum under very tough conditions with its excellent architectural quality and the precision with which it was built, using local materials and the hands of the craftspeople of Palestine. It gives the people the energy they need to sustain and continue regardless of the hardships and suffering that they go through.

View of the Palestinian Museum garden towards the sea

SARAH ZAHRAN

Sarah Zahran is the Yasmine and Laila Qaddumi Education Unit officer at the Palestinian Museum. Since its inception, the museum has offered a specialised educational programme with various activities geared towards school and university students and families. Sarah coordinates and leads the different activities, which include art workshops, interactive tours, and family days.
The educational programme is based on the institution's awareness of the importance of interactive education and is thus designed to spur creativity, critical thinking, and self-expression. It is meant to open the horizon for dialogue with the knowledge provided by the museum's exhibitions and programmes towards developing the skills of participants. This development is accomplished by motivating participants to critique and ask questions and by enhancing their means of self-expression. The educational programme offers space for participants to expand their individual and collective experiences through tools that make concepts more tangible, encouraging them to imagine, research, and discover.
The museum also organises summer programmes and activities for all ages that capture a wide audience. Across the different themes, these offerings strengthen museum culture for the upcoming generation and open possibilities for new visions that bring history straight to the heart, on learning paths based on the arts and their various tools. (EN)

Sarah Zahran
Reflecting on the Educational Programme at the Palestinian Museum

An Overview of the Educational Programme
The Palestinian Museum works to create summer programmes and activities for all ages that capture a wide audience, with interactive tours of the museum exhibitions, the garden, and the collection rooms. To this end, our activities are organised for the whole family and are created through a participatory methodology with contemporary tools that integrate history and art. In this way, a learning experience is created that goes above and beyond traditional learning methods. The different themes strengthen a museum culture for the upcoming generations and open up possibilities for a new vision of Palestinian history that goes straight to the heart – on a learning path based on the arts and their various tools.

On How the Different Spaces and Configurations Help the Various Educational Programmes
Different physical and digital platforms provide the museum audience with interactive educational materials developed to suit various inclusive needs, including animated videos, virtual reality, timeline interactive ports, and other materials that allow for engagement in the museum programme and exhibition, going beyond the typical school learning experience. The name Sanasel given to this educational platform[1] was inspired by the design and function of the museum and is linked to a learning process based on the construction of *sanasel*, the stonewall terraces that are so closely linked to Palestinian culture, the environment, and the people. The relationship with the surroundings is built from the basic components of the land, from the stones that farmers place atop one another with expertise, until they form a wall that protects the land from erosion and maintains its fertility. The museum learning process similarly occurs collectively and constructively, with each individual interacting and adding to it, so that an essay platform derives new meaning in jumping from the school wall to an open space of authentic learning.

On Particular Artworks That Attract More Attention
The first meeting between the visitors and the museum is dazzling. The fascination begins with the garden, where the roses are scattered along the sides, and with the beautiful design of the museum; the entrance with its high ceiling, which the kids love, comes across as a different space from the school. When they start wandering, kids love the place, especially the garden and terrace; they like to run and discover the surroundings. They are also attracted to the solar panels. The idea is to keep the place beautiful, clean, full of discoverable details. In my view, the most attractive artwork is

Students gathering in the Palestinian Museum's garden, transforming it into a communal space for their studies

Nida Sinnokrot's *Ka (Oslo)* from 2017 (two backhoe arms raised up to the skies in a primal gesture that recalls despair as well as prayer, absolution, and defiance). I find it to be a work that links contemporary art and culture, and it also helps visitors to understand the nature of the museum, both a historical cultural museum and a heritage one, though many people think only of the latter when the term 'museum' is mentioned. This building with its innovative design is similar to our dream in the educational programme of developing an innovative, free, authentic education for youth, through which we can create millions of possibilities.

1   https://sanasel.org

LARA ZUREIKAT

Lara Zureikat, a Jordanian landscape architect based in Amman, designed the gardens of the Palestinian Museum, as part of the overall team led by heneghan peng architects. When her work began in 2012, Zureikat was only able to visit the grounds of the hilly site on the campus of Birzeit University once. For the rest of the project's development and realisation, and until this day, she has not yet seen her garden design come to fruition. Being denied access meant that she has continued to work remotely, relying on close cooperation with the architects and workers on site. Regardless of these obstacles, Zureikat envisioned the gardens as a place rooted in Palestine traditions.
As in her other work to date, Zureikat continuously advocates for the sensitive deployment of native plants to compliment a site both conceptually and ecologically. By contributing to the museum a garden design closely linked to the site and its cultural history, Zureikat incorporated an insider's point of view into the overall landscaping project, as she currently continues to collaborate with the institution on its further development and follow its growth from afar. (EN)

Lara Zureikat
Reflecting on the Garden Design

On the Garden Design Concept and Collaboration with heneghan peng architects
The idea was to design the bones of a landscape that could be augmented over time. Just like the collection of the museum may grow with time, so can the collection of plants where new species and new plants can be added by the occupants and people using the gardens. The collaboration with heneghan peng architects and their design team was very interesting because it combined two different perspectives: that of an outsider seeing the landscape with a fresh eye, and a more intimate perspective of someone familiar with the details of the landscape and its cultural significance. We worked very collaboratively, especially because the landscape is an extension of the building, and the two elements were designed to follow the same cohesive scheme, weaving into each other both spatially and conceptually.

On References of Inspiration and the Final Design Layout
My references for the project were really my observations: on the one hand, observing the native landscapes of Palestine, especially in the Mediterranean bioregion where the project is located and, on the other, observing the cultural landscape and how people shaped the land over time and how they dealt with topography. I was fortunate enough to be able to see many traditional villages first hand, in both Palestine and Jordan. The landscapes are very similar, as there's no geographic borders when it comes to plants. They don't know any political boundaries, so experiencing those landscapes really helped shape the design and inform a lot of the decisions that were made. Other references involved speaking with elder members of my family. People who really experienced the farming landscape and had a much more intimate relationship with it. They lived it; they did rain-fed agriculture on the hillsides. It was really important to speak to people with that first-hand knowledge. The garden is organised around a series of terraces that adapt to the terrain and take the visitor on a journey, from the upper area where the building stands to the lowest point in the garden. The terraces are populated with a variety of culturally significant trees that form different orchards along them. There are olive orchards interplanted with rain-fed wheat, representing a historically important traditional crop in Palestine. They lead to a terrace with pomegranate trees interplanted with chickpeas, the main ingredient in the typical dish of hummus. On the lower terraces, there is a collection of fruit trees that are important for many traditional desserts, such as walnuts, pistachios, different traditional nut trees, along with apricots and mulberries. Another idea was actually representing the seasons and the strong cultural connection to the seasons. For example, seeing almond blossoms or eating fresh almond fruit signals spring to the people of Palestine, so the garden is populated by various species, each connected to the different seasons.

The garden merging into the landscape

Looking at different plants and how they culturally relate to the place was also important; I researched medicinal plants and their traditional uses. There's a pathway in the garden called the aromatic walk. It takes you from the upper to the lower terraces and connects the entire series of garden spaces together. This pathway is lined with aromatic plants such as sage, mint, lemon verbina, and zaatar (oregano), as well as many other herbs that are used in traditional cooking and folk medicine. Everyone in Palestine has had their grandmother prescribe sage to cure stomach-aches, so it was important to include these plants to signify and connect to their cultural significance and also to celebrate the common plants that we find all around us in a museum setting.

On the Outcome and Being Denied Access to See It
Looking at the final design, there's a clear structure to the landscape that communicates the cultural and natural heritage of Palestine but at the same time leaves room for people to add to the landscape. It was the design intention to have a canvas that can be added to. Over time a lot of artworks and installations have already been introduced, and it's really nice to see how those different additions are working with the existing canvas.
Having been denied access to the site during construction was very difficult. Landscape work needs a lot of direct contact with the site, both during and after construction, in order to have a first-hand view of how the plants grow and to have that direct dialogue with the institution about how to progress with developing the landscape over time. That, up until now, has happened mostly through remote means. We haven't been able to actually go and see the finished product, but we do continue our work with the institution to progress the landscape.

The Birth of the Museum
Shadia Touqan
Beshara Doumani
Nabil Qaddumi
Omar Al-Qattan

The Palestinian Museum's Creation Process
Shadia Touqan

Taawon board members had been debating the notion of building a Palestinian Museum since the late 1990s. In 1998, a special committee was formed to discuss the necessary specifics, realistic next steps, logistical considerations, and potential financing to enable the realisation of this museum project which was intended to tell the story of Palestine's past and present – thus indicating the Palestinian Museum's 'birth' in official terms (fig. 1).

The birth of the Palestinian Museum, however, was followed by a protracted and complex process of 'labour', as Taawon had to carefully weigh all of the choices for the implementation of the museum. This was due to the peculiar circumstances surrounding its location, the overall political situation, and the background for establishing such a museum. Decisions had to be made regarding the nature and features of the museum and how it would most effectively depict and communicate Palestine's story.

Participation

As a member of the Palestinian Museum committee, I became involved from the project's inception in 1998 and continued to be a part of it until 2014.

I served on the jury in the 2011 international design competition for the Palestinian Museum, which was won by heneghan peng architects. I also took part in the design development group's assessment and discussions with the architect Róisín Heneghan and her team until the final design was accepted for implementation (figs. 2 and 3).

The Birth (Phase 1, 1998 to 2011)

Numerous topics needed to be examined, decided upon, and subsequently debated with the Taawon board of trustees throughout this protracted process. This phase also included holding several workshops and seminars with the participation of Palestinian stakeholders and local and international experts in relevant fields.

Taawon remained adamant throughout the meetings and discussions that the future planning must proceed despite the ongoing unpredictability in Palestine. The discussion covered various

Figure 1. Information board introducing the construction

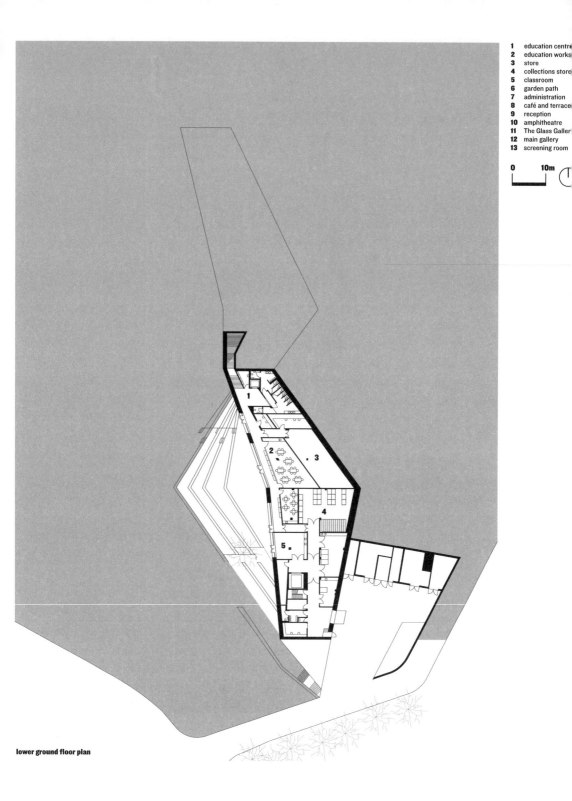

Figure 2. Palestinian Museum, ground floor plan

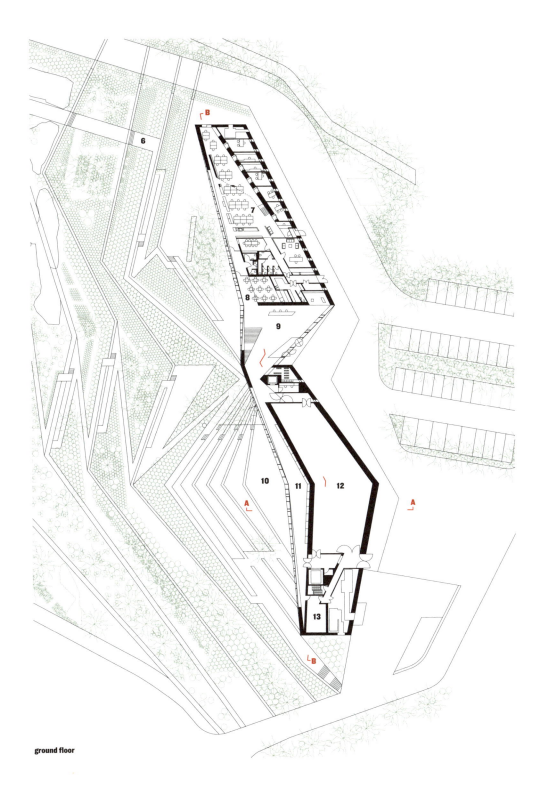

ground floor

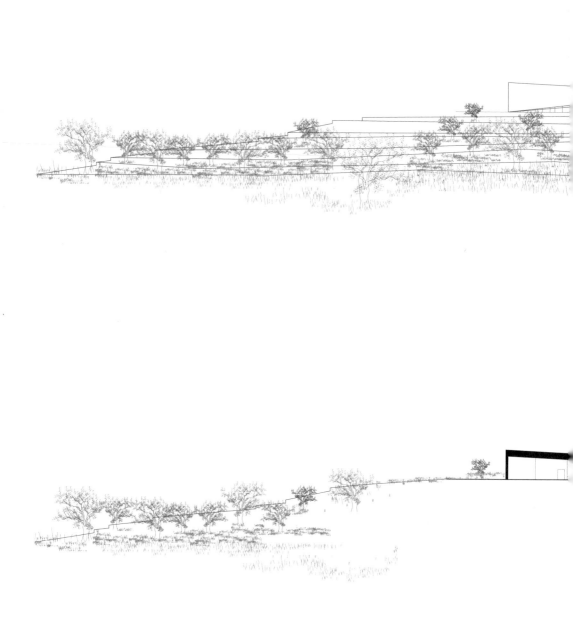

Figure 3. Palestinian Museum, long section

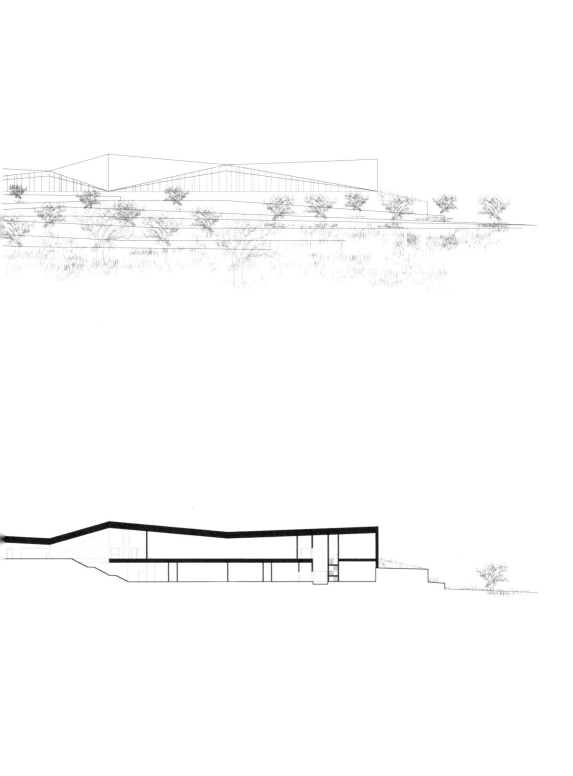

scenarios to get around the obstacles and limitations by being innovative, adaptable, and taking advantage of all available technological resources, as well as being open to new international trends in museum design and management.

The following primary crucial factors were considered throughout the project's initial phase:

- **What** aspect of the Palestinian Museum's narrative (historical, political, cultural, anthropological, etc.) should be the main focus? What period of Palestinian history should the content of the Palestinian Museum reflect? The museum's original name was the Palestinian Memory Museum, but the 'Memory' was eliminated since it was perceived as constrictive and suggested a sole concentration on history and the past (figs. 4 and 5).

- **How** can the fragmented and dispersed Palestinian nation be represented, involved in the museum's construction, and benefit from it? (Palestinians living in various regions of the occupied country, Palestinians living in refugee camps in neighbouring Arab countries since 1948, and Palestinian diaspora who have voluntarily or involuntarily moved overseas.)

- In **what location** would the Palestinian Museum building be? Different scenarios were investigated while taking the intricate logistics and challenging accessibility into account. But Jerusalem was always the preferred choice. There were several places and plots of land

Figures 4 and 5. Views of the exhibition *A People by the Sea: Narratives of the Palestinian Coast*, 2021–23

Figure 6. View from above in the early stages of construction

available; however, after the various options were explored, it was determined that because Jerusalem is still occupied, the authorities will never issue a building permit for such a museum. Consequently, it was decided to build the Palestinian Museum in the West Bank as a close alternative that should give some accessibility to Palestinians from this area. Finally, it was agreed to build it on land adjacent to Birzeit University that had been semi-donated by the university (fig. 6).

- **What** would be the nature of the museum's collections, acquisitions, and exhibits and what would they be focused on? And how may that affect what might be moved to or from Palestine, or even from other Palestinian territories, given its restricted geographical accessibility? Nevertheless, with rapidly advancing technology around the turn of the century, plans for geographical expansion through the establishment of sub-museums outside Palestine or cooperation with regional and worldwide museums were taken into consideration. More recently, the Palestinian Museum has benefited from technology by adopting virtual technology for training, exhibitions, and other purposes.

Figure 7. The Palestinian Museum arising from the limestone hill

The Realisation (Phase 2, 2011-17)

As a member of the Palestinian Museum committee until 2014, I participated in earlier years of this phase as a member of the competition design jury (2011) and in the design development group (2012-14).

The Role of the Palestinian Museum among Designers and Those Involved in the Preservation of Palestinian Heritage

Protection of culture and cultural heritage has been and continues to be an integral part of the Palestinian struggle for independence and liberation. Through the years and decades of occupation, Palestinians continue to promote and practise various components of their cultural traditions (art, music, crafts, literature, poetry, etc.), while preserving and revitalising Palestine's natural and cultural heritage (tangible and intangible). Culture is considered the witness of Palestinian history, identity, and individuality, reflecting their past and claiming their future.

For young Palestinian professionals working in the culture sector and in the preservation of heritage in Palestine, the impact of the museum's establishment, architecture, landscape, content, and activities cannot yet be assessed. In time, it may be useful to consider a study or survey on the subject.

Figure 8. Structural framework of the Palestinian Museum embedded in the landscape

The architectural and landscape design of the Palestinian Museum, however, has opened discussions and arguments among the younger local architects. The Palestinian Museum design has offered a different model, at a time when young, new graduates are witnessing the more brutally constructed settlements that dominate the tops of Palestinian hills, which have been seized from their owners, and also the inappropriately designed and constructed modern commercial architecture by local architectural firms. In both cases, the structures have been built to satisfy commercial or political goals, disregarding the damage that will be caused to the traditional architecture and the environment.

From the various views and comments, most agreed that the approach of the Palestinian Museum design demonstrated a new style that was mindful of the surroundings and advocated for a more compassionate design – one that complements the land and the Palestinians' traditional use of it for agriculture by blending in with the site topography rather than dominating it (figs. 7 and 8). The design was obviously the result of an in-depth appreciation for, and grasp of, the architectural, environmental, topographical, political, and human components required by such a project, offering a different example for local practitioners to consider.

Figure 9. Construction machines working on the stony terrain

As to the public, many appreciated that the building's design skilfully balanced the strong Palestinian stone with the land's terraced terrain, while enhancing and complimenting the vibrant greenery of the surrounding rural area. Many appreciated the Herb Garden, which is incorporated into the landscape design, unifying the interior space of the museum with the exterior space that provides the livelihood offered by the landscape. The building was designed to look as though it were naturally growing from Palestinian earth in order to provide a suitable container for the various chapters of Palestine's cultural, natural, and historical story (fig. 9).

At this time of global concern about environmental deterioration and global warming, practitioners, including young local architects, new graduates, and university architecture students, have also recognised the importance of the design's emphasis on solving environmental needs while creating a green building.

Palestinians in general, and young architects in particular, felt proud, encouraged, and hopeful when the project received the Aga Khan Award for Architecture in 2019. The museum evolved into a role model to be followed.

SHADIA TOUQAN holds a BSc in architecture from Cairo University, an MA in urban design from Manchester University, and a PhD in urban planning and development from the Bartlett Development Planning Unit, University College London. From 1998 until 2014, she was involved in the project's inception as a member of the Palestinian Museum committee. After serving as a jury member during the international design competition for the Palestinian Museum in 2011, she collaborated closely with the winners, heneghan peng architects, during the design process.

A Walk Up the Hill: Reflections on the Palestinian Museum's Place and Space
Beshara Doumani

It was with decidedly mixed emotions that I started my walk up the hill being considered as the site for the Palestinian Museum. I had spent the previous two years leading a team to develop a strategic plan espousing a vision that radically departed from the original idea of a traditional narrative museum. The new vision – a transnational cultural mobilisation project rooted in the land of Palestine but encompassing all Palestinians – required innovating the museum form to meet the needs of a stateless and spatially fragmented people engaged in a struggle for freedom, justice, equality, and right of return to their homeland. This meant, among many other things, investing more in human resources than in space and place, and focusing more on weaving an interactive network of regional and global partners than on acquiring and preserving permanent collections. After all, the museum project had to be implemented under conditions of settler colonialism and apartheid. There is no shortage of examples of Israeli military raids that looted Palestinian civil society institutions over the past decades. Besides, the system of severe restrictions on mobility imposed by the Israeli military meant that only relatively few Palestinians could visit the museum.

I confess that I delayed discussions on the building and location as much as possible. Unlike many of the museum's biggest supporters who considered it the most important part of the project, I envisioned the museum grounds more as the supporting cast than the star; a humble beehive of creativity rather than a grand architectural statement that marvels at itself. But the moment had come: a spot had to be chosen and there were architectural options to consider. What would be the guiding principle behind both? That is the big question that haunted me as I reached the summit of the limestone hill under a glaring sun anchoring a clear blue sky (fig. 10).

The repetitive movement during the walk between fine-grained and sweeping scales of vision – eyes down as I navigated the rock-strewn landscape filled with wild thyme and thorny bushes, then eyes up to follow the gentle West-facing slope pointing to the glimmering Mediterranean Sea at the edge of the horizon – made the obvious clear. Just as the concept of the museum had to be stretched and bent to do decolonial work, the architecture and landscape had to humble themselves. They had to become one with a nondescript hill in a rural area far from Jerusalem, the symbolically (and tourist) saturated capital long considered the natural place for a museum of this scale and ambition.

Figure 10. View of the stone walls terracing the garden, leading up to the Palestinian Museum

The deference and respect to the quotidian required of the structure and grounds to become one with this mound of limestone would, ironically, allow them to tell the most important story of the Palestinian condition. Namely, the relationship of people to the land or, more accurately, the relationship among people about land. If the former speaks of indigeneity and belonging, the latter reveals the internal hierarchies, power struggles, and contradictions of Palestinian society and history: the very stuff that makes the material culture of everyday life a fertile ground for curatorial practices that deepen understanding, challenge assumptions, and imagine potential futures.

To be one with the hill recognises that Palestinian stories are literally archived in stone in ways that exceed the colonial frame. Long before Zionist settlement and British colonial occupation, to belong to the land was also to struggle with others over land. How to allow the stone to speak

and narrate our stories? A low limestone building – straddling the top of the hill and giving way to terraces of indigenous fauna and flora – can become a gateway, a sanctuary, and a stage for curated liberatory acts of return to the land; albeit, acts devoid of nostalgia and romance; acts untainted by modernist pretensions; and acts that refuse to be shoehorned into nationalist constructions of the past or limited to state-based visions of the future. Only such curatorial practices, deeply rooted in the soil yet with an expansive view towards what seems to be an impossible horizon, are capable of paving alternative and globally resonant paths to being and becoming; not just with ourselves and with others, but also with stone, seeds, and animals.

Beshara Doumani is the Mahmoud Darwish Professor of Palestinian Studies at Brown University, the former president of Birzeit University in Palestine, and the founding director of the Palestinian Museum. This essay benefited from conversations with his daughter, Yara Doumani, who is currently working on Palestinian museological practices.

The Palestinian Museum: Journey of a Dream
Nabil Qaddumi

The establishment of Taawon (previously the Welfare Association), a Palestinian non-profit foundation, forty years ago in 1983 went hand in hand with its founders' cherished idea and dream of establishing a Palestinian Museum. But not until 1997 did the board of trustees launch the idea of the 'Palestinian Remembrance Museum' with a determination to establish it in Jerusalem.

Finding suitable land in Jerusalem was a big challenge; and the realisation that it was impossible to establish a museum in a city controlled by the occupation forces took years to sink in.

As a two-term chairman of the board of trustees during the period from 2008 to 2014, my colleagues and I were able to reach an agreement with Birzeit University, where the university designated an area of just under 40 dunams or 4 hectares for the establishment of the museum (fig. 11).

It is an exceptional site at the highest point of the university campus with a commanding position over the landscape. Long-range views offered the opportunity to develop designs that capture the Palestinian landscape with vistas that include the Mediterranean Sea.

On 21 November 2009, the board of trustees – during its 57th meeting in London – approved my decision to form a museum task force to develop a strategic plan for the museum. This plan took into consideration technological and artistic advancements in the development of museums and included an action plan with a budget leading to the museum's design and the kick-off of its construction processes.

A year later, at the board of trustee's 59th meeting in Amman, Jordan, held on 12 November 2010, the board approved both the task force's report on the museum's concept and the required budget for its execution during the various project phases. At that meeting, US$2 million were raised through the contributions of several board members.

Figure 11. View of the construction site of the Palestinian Museum

In the strategic plan, the museum's vision was articulated as a mobilising cultural project that acts as an agent of empowerment, integration, and international solidarity. Its mission is to become the leading and the most credible and robust platform for shaping and communicating knowledge about Palestinian history, society, and culture.

The Palestinian Museum was to be conceived as a transnational institution driven by an intellectual mission to provide the authoritative cultural voice for Palestinians worldwide through physical and virtual mediums.

After twelve months of detailed strategic planning, the Palestinian Museum task force of Taawon agreed in May 2011 to proceed with a formal process to select an architect to work with the Palestinian Museum team to develop the master plan and Phase 1 design for the Palestinian Museum.

Figure 12. Guests attend the ceremony of the unveiling of the 'inaugural stone' of the new Palestinian Museum

Following a pre-qualification process involving over forty invited firms, five architects were shortlisted and invited to submit proposals by 22 November 2011. They were also invited to give formal presentations on 2-3 December 2011 in London to the steering committee and advisory panel, which included Taawon members of the Palestinian Museum task force, stakeholders, and experts.

The review by the steering committee and the advisory panel provided Taawon's museum task force with a recommendation for the selected architect.

The Palestinian Museum task force endorsed this recommendation on 9 December 2011, and the board of trustees approved it on 16 December 2011 during their Amman meeting.

The architect submitted the schematic design documents on 17 August 2012, which were subsequently reviewed in September 2012 by the project manager.

The Palestinian Museum 'inaugural stone' was laid on the museum's site in Birzeit in May 2013, in a ceremony attended by board of trustees members, stakeholders, and friends (fig. 12).

Taawon finally was on track to deliver its dream of the Palestinian Museum, securing members, supporters, and institutional funds to cover the costs of its construction and subsequent operation.

Taawon collaborated with other institutions, organisations, and individuals to bring the museum project to fruition. This included working closely with Palestinian and international cultural and historical experts and architects, as well as implementing cultural and educational programmes.

Taawon also succeeded in supporting the Palestinian Museum building with its institutional capacity and the expertise required for operating a world-class museum. This involved supporting the training of museum staff, curators, and educators to ensure the effective management and functioning of the institution.

In 2016, the Palestinian Museum opened its doors, and the first on-site exhibition took place in 2017.

Since then, five other major exhibitions were held and a number of initiatives launched, including a bilingual interactive encyclopedia of the Palestine question, the Palestinian Museum Digital Archive (which today holds around 300,000 documents, photographs, and films in its collection), the ever-expanding education and outreach programme, and the first Arab museum website for children.

Today, as the current Taawon chairman, I look back with pride on a journey built on a dream that culminated in a major cultural flagship manifested as the Palestinian Museum.

Nabil Qaddumi accompanied the project in the position of chairman of the board of trustees for the Welfare Association (Taawon). Since 1983, the Welfare Association has been serving as a non-profit organisation and, in 1997, initiated the Palestinian Museum project, with the aim of building a commemorative museum that could mark the 50th anniversary of the Nakba.

Some Lessons Learnt: The Palestinian Museum
Omar Al-Qattan

Having accompanied the Palestinian Museum project since its inception, I have learnt many lessons, some surprising but some rather blindingly obvious (with the benefit of hindsight).

Sometimes we think we see clarity behind a cloudy sky because of a few stunning rays of light that give us hope and courage. And suddenly the darkness obscures the rays and we are left in despair.

Thus, before we opened the Palestinian Museum, we were confident that we could create a 'thematic museum' without an initial core collection, and that people would understand the idea (it would surely become clear to the public sooner or later, we were certain!). We believed that we could inaugurate a beautiful building and make it work as a functioning museum without having enough trained staff in the country (they would come in due course!). And, perhaps most naively, we gave little consideration to the powerful Israeli military occupation of our country, though it hampers everything.

All of these difficulties I would rather not have had to deal with. Yet after we inaugurated the stunning Palestinian Museum building in May 2016, our false assumptions exposed us to doubt and criticism, some of it scornful, racist, and condescending, but some of it well-meaning and from friendlier quarters. It was very sobering and it has taken several years of extremely hard work and determination to finally silence these doubts, forever I hope.

This said, I wonder if we would have ever created the Palestinian Museum had we been clearer in our thinking! Perhaps we would have dithered far too long and finally given up? I believe this sort of crazy project requires a degree of blind faith and naivety for it ever to become a reality.

That may be the sweetest lesson I have learnt.

Another vital lesson I learnt is that you will *always and forever* need more modular, flexible spaces than you think. Practicality is just as important as an aesthetic pleading for beauty (fig. 13).

Figure 13: The Palestinian Museum's spaces illuminated during the night

Naturally, many challenges continue to haunt us – that we will run out of financial support or lose the popular goodwill; that we are in too volatile a part of the world for people and institutions to entrust their objects to our care; that we are too ambitious and sophisticated to be accessible and popular; that we have no government to protect us; and, perhaps most seriously, that a new catastrophe might befall our beautiful country and people, leading inevitably to the museum's disappearance. But yet again, it is courage and determination, rather than rational analysis, that will help us to keep this project alive, although this time round, we will certainly be better armed by the harsh lessons learnt from our foolhardy and faltering beginnings.

Omar Al-Qattan has been a part of the Palestinian Museum task force since 1998 and chaired its first board of directors (2020-23) as an independent institution. He is one of its most dedicated supporters. His second, and last, term as chair ends in 2026.

Contributor Biographies

Nadi Abusaada is an architect and a historian. He is currently a postdoctoral fellow in the Institute for the History and Theory of Architecture (GTA) at the Department of Architecture, ETH Zürich. Abusaada received his PhD and MPhil degrees from the University of Cambridge and his BA (Hons) from the University of Toronto.
Before moving to Zurich, he was an Aga Khan Postdoctoral Fellow in the School of Architecture + Planning at the Massachusetts Institute of Technology (MIT). Abusaada is also the co-founder of Arab Urbanism, a global network dedicated to historical and contemporary urban issues in the Arab region. His writings have been featured in international publications including *The Architectural Review, The International Journal of Islamic Architecture,* and the *Jerusalem Quarterly.*

Amin Alsaden is a curator, writer, and educator. He holds a doctoral degree from Harvard University, a master's degree from Princeton University, and completed his undergraduate education at the American University of Sharjah.
Alsaden has taught at several institutions, at both the graduate and undergraduate levels, and regularly serves as an invited lecturer, critic, and jury member at art, curatorial, and design programs. Alsaden's research explores the history and theory of modern and contemporary art and architecture globally, with specific expertise in the Arab and Muslim worlds. He has published and lectured widely. In 2018, he was the director of the Sharjah Architecture Triennale and, from 2019 to 2021, was the Nancy McCain and Bill Morneau Curatorial Fellow at The Power Plant Contemporary Art Gallery.

Elias Anastas is a French-Palestinian architect and designer. He studied architecture at l'Ecole d'architecture de Paris Val de Seine where he received a master's degree in 2007. In 2009, he won the first prize for the Edward Said National Conservatory in Bethlehem and, back in Bethlehem, followed the construction of the project. In 2014, he was honoured with the 'Europe 40under40' award for young European architects. In 2011, Elias founded Local Industries, a project born from the desire to put direct collaboration with local artisans at the heart of the process and to look for ways to minimise energy consumption for the creation and production of industrial design.

Yousef Anastas is a French-Palestinian architect and engineer. He studied architecture at l'Ecole d'architecture de la ville et des territoires, where he received a master's degree in 2011. He pursued a degree in civil engineering and graduated from l'Ecole Nationale des Ponts et Chaussees in 2014.

That same year, he conducted research at the Form Finding Lab of Princeton University on biomimetic building skins. In 2014, he was awarded the 'Europe 40under40' award for young European architects. He is currently leading AAU Anastas' research department, SCALES, which is a research laboratory that is consistently enhanced by linking scales that are otherwise opposed.

Mirna Bamieh is an artist. She obtained a BA in psychology from Birzeit University, Ramallah (2006) and an MFA from the Bezalel Academy for Arts and Design, Jerusalem (2013), Ashkal Alwan Homeworks Study Program, Beirut (2014).
With a degree in the culinary arts, in 2018 Bamieh founded Palestine Hosting Society, a live art project. She has taken part in several art residencies, including Binz 39, Zurich (2022), The Invisible Dog Art Center, New York (2021), Vooruit, Belgium (2020), Ujazdowski Castle Centre for Contemporary Art, Poland (2019), Tokyo Wonder Site, Japan (2016), Maroc Artist Meeting, Marrakech (2016), Art Omi, New York (2015), and Delfina Foundation, London (2012). Bamieh's grants and awards include: Dr Georg and Josi Guggenheim Foundation Award, Zurich (2022), CEC ArtsLink International Fellowship, New York (2020), The Visible Project Award (long list), Paris (2017), and the A. M. Qattan Foundation Grant (2012, 2013, 2014).

Meisa Batayneh is an architect and the founder and principal at maisam architects & engineers, based in Amman, Jordan. Batayneh studied architecture at the University of Texas at Arlington, prior to leading multidisciplinary teams on large-scale international and regional projects in the United States, Pakistan, Cyprus, Saudi Arabia, Egypt, and the United Arab Emirates. Batayneh is a member of the advisory committees of the Jordanian Ministry of Environment, the Amman Commission, and the Architecture & Engineering Business Council. She is the chairperson of Design Jordan, president of Business & Professional Women of Amman (BPW-A), and vice president of the Jordan Federation for Business & Professional Women. She has served as a member of the 2022 and 2025 Steering Committee of the Aga Khan Award for Architecture and a member of the Master Jury in 2019.
She was a member of the Global Holcim Awards jury (2015 and 2021), a member of the Holcim Awards jury for Middle East Africa (2017 and 2023), and joined the Board of the Holcim Foundation for Sustainable Construction in 2020.

Tomà Berlanda, architect and educator, is a professor of architectural technology at the Politecnico di Torino, and an honorary research associate at the University of Cape Town, where he served as professor (2015-23) and director (2015-18) of the School of Architecture, Planning and Geomatics. Berlanda holds a PhD in architecture from the Politecnico di Torino, and a diploma in architecture from the Accademia di Architettura in Mendrisio. He has taught at numerous institutions, including Syracuse University, Cornell University, and the Kigali Institute of Science and Technology. He served as an on-site review member of the Aga Khan Award for Architecture in the 2016 and 2019 cycles.

Farrokh Derakhshani is the director of the Aga Khan Award for Architecture and has been associated with the Award since 1982. Derakhshani trained as an architect and planner at the National University of Iran and later continued his studies at the School of Architecture in Paris (UP1). His main field of specialisation is the contemporary architecture of Muslim societies. He lectures widely and has organised and participated in numerous international seminars, exhibitions, colloquia, workshops, and international competitions. He has served as a jury member at various international competitions and schools of architecture and collaborated on a large variety of architecture-related publications.

Róisín Heneghan is an architect and co-founder of heneghan peng architects along with Shi-Fu Peng. The company was established in New York in 1999 but was shifted to Dublin in 2001. In 2014, she was shortlisted for *Architects' Journal*'s Woman Architect of the Year. Heneghan received a Bachelor of Architecture (1987) from the University College of Dublin and a Master of Architecture from Harvard University.
Taking a multidisciplinary approach to design, the team collaborates extensively with renowned designers and engineers on various projects, spanning urban master plans, bridges, landscapes, and buildings. Current endeavours include the construction of the Storm King Art Center visitor and support buildings in New York and the temporary exhibition pavilions at Trinity College Dublin. Awards received by the practice include the Aga Khan Award for Architecture (2019) and the RIBA European Award for Áras Chill Dara 2006.

Walter J. Hood is a landscape architect and educator. He is Chair and Professor of Landscape Architecture & Environmental Planning and Urban Design at the UC Berkeley College of Environmental Design, as well as the creative director and founder of Hood Design Studio in Oakland, CA.
Hood holds a distinguished MFA from the School of the Art Institute of Chicago, a dual MLA and MArch degree from the University of California, Berkeley, and a BLA from North Carolina A&T State University. He has been the recipient of various accolades: the Academy of Arts and Letters Architecture Award (2017), Knight Public Spaces Fellowship (2019), MacArthur Fellowship (2019), Dorothy and Lillian Gish Prize (2019), and the Architectural League's President's Medal (2021).

Alexandre Kazerouni is a scholar, currently Maître de conférences en sociologie politique at the Département Géographie et Territoires of the École normale supérieure in Paris. He holds a doctorate in political sciences, with a concentration on the Muslim world, from the Institut d'études politiques de Paris (Sciences Po), as well as a degree in mining engineering from the École nationale supérieure des Mines in Nancy. He has been a researcher at the Centre Jean Pépin (CNRS), Responsable de la mineure Géopolitique & Diplomatie du Département Géographie et Territoires (ENS) since 2019, and Responsable du parcours de master Programme Moyen-Orient Méditerranée (Université Paris Sciences et Lettres, ENS) between 2019 and 2021.

Adrian Lahoud is an architect, urban designer, and researcher. He is the dean of the School of Architecture at the Royal College of Art, London, and co-chair of the Rights of Future Generations Working Group. He holds a PhD from the University of Technology in Sydney. Lahoud has been studio master in the programme Projective Cities, Architectural Association, London, and director of the MA in research architecture, Goldsmiths, University of London. He has also worked as a researcher on the Forensic Architecture ERC grant at Goldsmiths as part of their collaboration with Amnesty International on the Gaza Platform.
Lahoud was the inaugural curator of the Sharjah Architecture Triennial (2019). His work has also been presented in exhibitions such as *Let's Talk about the Weather: Art and Ecology in a Time of Crisis,* Sursock Museum, Beirut (2016), *After Belonging,* Oslo Architecture Triennale (2016), and *Forensis: The Architecture of Public Truth,* Haus der Kulturen der Welt, Berlin (2014).

Adila Laïdi-Hanieh is a writer, scholar, and curator who served as the director general of the Palestinian Museum in Birzeit between 2018 and 2023. She holds a doctorate in cultural studies from George Mason University in Virginia. Laïdi-Hanieh published the artist biography *Fahrelnissa Zeid: Painter of Inner Worlds* in 2017, and the first cultural review of contemporary Palestine in 2008, *Palestine: Rien ne nous manque ici* (Palestine: We Lack for Nothing Here). She has taught Arab intellectual history, and the first course on Palestinian arts at Birzeit University from 2006 to 2008, and was the founding director of the Khalil Sakakini Cultural Centre in Ramallah from 1996 until 2005. Laïdi-Hanieh received the French Chevalier de l'Ordre national du Mérite in 2023.

Ella Neumaier is a doctoral candidate in the Laboratory of the History and Theories of Architecture, Media, and Technology (HITAM) at the École Polytechnique Fédérale de Lausanne with an interest in intercontinental transfers of goods, labor, and knowledge. Neumaier holds an MA in architecture (cultural heritage, history, and criticism) from the Technical University of Munich (TUM) and is an editorial advisor to the Berlin-based publishing house ArchiTangle. Before joining HITAM, she was a curatorial assistant to numerous exhibition projects at Munich's Architekturmuseum der TUM in the Pinakothek der Moderne, including *Who's Next? Homelessness, Architecture, and Cities* (2021). In 2022, she curated the 20th anniversary exhibition of the Pinakothek der Moderne.

Raja Shehadeh is a lawyer, human rights activist, and writer. He studied English literature at the American University of Beirut and law at the College of Law in London. In 1979, Shehadeh co-founded the award-winning Palestinian human rights organisation Al-Haq. He is the author of several books on international law, human rights, and the Middle East, including *Occupiers Law* and *From Occupation to Interim Accords*. His literary books include *Strangers in the House: Coming of Age in Occupied Palestine*; *Occupation Diaries*; *A Rift in Time: Travels with My Ottoman Uncle*; *Language of War, Language of Peace*; *Palestinian Walks: Forays into a Vanishing Landscape*, which won the 2008 Orwell Prize; *Where the Line Is Drawn: Crossing Boundaries in Occupied Palestine*; and *Going Home: A Walk Through Fifty Years of Occupation*. His latest book is *We Could Have Been Friends My Father and I: A Palestinian Memoir*, which has been longlisted for the 2023 National Book Award for Nonfiction in New York.

Cristina Steingräber is the founder of ArchiTangle, a publisher focused on socially engaged architectural practice and urbanism. Her academic and professional efforts focus on interdisciplinary knowledge transfer on how architecture can engage with other disciplines in shaping the built environment. Steingräber, initially a curator at the Nationalgalerie, Staatliche Museen zu Berlin (SMB), was later appointed head of the SMB's publications department in 2004. Thereafter, Steingräber served as programme director and CEO of the leading global art publisher Hatje Cantz (2006–17). She holds a PhD in art and architectural history from Kiel University (CAU) alongside an MBA in economic sciences from the Technical University of Munich (TUM). Steingräber is frequently engaged as an invited lecturer, critic, and jury member within the fields of art and architecture.

Hanan Toukan is a professor of Middle East studies at Bard College Berlin. She completed her PhD in social sciences at SOAS, University of London. Toukan was previously a visiting assistant professor of Middle East studies and history of art at Brown University and a visiting professor of cultural studies of the Middle East at Bamberg University. She is also a recipient of several research awards, including, most recently, from the Alexander von Humboldt Foundation. Toukan is the author of *The Politics of Art: Dissent and Cultural Diplomacy in Lebanon, Palestine, and Jordan* published by Stanford University Press (2021).

Sarah Zahran is the Yasmine and Laila Qaddumi Education Unit officer at the Palestinian Museum. Interested in the arts as tools for learning and knowledge, she has authored contributions, stories, and articles in the fields of literature, sociology, and learning pedagogy. She has held positions as project supervisor at the Tamer Foundation for Community Education and as a teaching assistant at Birzeit University, where she earned a master's degree in sociology.

Lara Zureikat is a landscape architect and the associate director at the Center for the Study of the Built Environment (CSBE), Amman, Jordan. She holds a master's degree in landscape architecture from the University of California, Berkeley, and a bachelor's degree in architecture from the University of Notre Dame. Zureikat's work at CSBE focuses on the design of native, water-conserving landscapes. She designed the first model water-conserving park for the Jordan National Gallery of Fine Arts and led an extensive public resource and publication programme promoting the use of drought-tolerant flora in landscape design. She was a recipient of the 2019 Aga Khan Award for Architecture for the Palestinian Museum, Birzeit. She also served as an on-site review member of the 2022 Aga Khan Award for Architecture.

Acknowledgements

I owe a particular debt of gratitude to Farrokh Derakhshani, director of the Aga Khan Award for Architecture, for inviting me to serve as an on-site reviewer for the Award, which enabled me to visit the Palestinian Museum in the spring of 2019. Little did I know back then that the seeds planted with that first encounter, and the many friendships and conversations it has allowed me to nurture over the years, would grow into the editorial project of this book. If anything, my first impression of the institution was that it was not simply part of a shifting landscape but an agent of change. Wrapping up the book at a dark and terrible time for the life of Palestinians, one cannot but recognise the wisdom of His Highness, the Aga Khan, and the Steering Committee and Master Jury he convened for the Award, as being an integral part of the hope that the volume calls to mind.

I would like to thank all of the contributors for their deep dedication and commitment to this project. The initial conceptualisation of the book happened as part of close conversations with Farrokh Derakhshani and Nadia Siméon (AKAA), Cristina Steingräber (ArchiTangle), Róisín Heneghan (hparc), Lara Zureikat (LZLA), and Adila Laïdi-Hanieh (Palestinian Museum). The fertile exchange and the participation in the brainstorming sessions were invaluable in assisting and refining the conceptual framework. The editorial process would have not been possible without Ella Neumaier's special dedication and commitment. Special thanks are due also to the other members of the team at ArchiTangle, including Marlene Schneider, Dawn Michelle d'Atri for copyediting, and Julia Wagner for graphic design. Mohammad al-Asad provided invaluable feedback.

In Birzeit I would like to extend a particular debt of gratitude to all the staff of the Palestinian Museum, for their unwavering generosity and support, as well as the larger community of friends and stakeholders of the institution that have played, and continue to play, a pivotal role in its existence, resistance, and growth.

The editorial project coincided with a major transition in my own life, as I transferred from the University of Cape Town, South Africa, to the Politecnico di Torino, Italy. Across this journey, the support of my family was a precious anchor to hold on to, and I feel privileged to be able to share these roots of hope with them.

Tomà Berlanda

Image Credits

All copyrights belong to the respective owners listed below, to whom we are grateful for the honour of presenting their work in this book.

Unless otherwise noted, heneghan peng architects have provided all the drawings and hold the copyright for their material.

Rana Abushkhaidem / The Palestinian Museum: pp. 4–5, 124, 144–45, 202; Aga Khan Trust for Culture / Cemal Emden: pp. cover, 17, 29, 126 (left), 175, 179; Aga Khan Trust for Culture / Les Studios Casagrande: p. 177; Aga Khan Trust for Culture / Hareth Yousef: pp. 173 (film still), 183 (film still); M.Ahmadani / Wikimedia Commons, Creative Commons Attribution-Share Alike 4.0 International license, https://commons.wikimedia.org/wiki/File:Photograph_of_the_area_of_the_Sharjah_Art_Foundation.jpg: p. 39; Elias and Yousef Anastas / AAU ANASTAS: p. 91; Iwan Baan: pp. 96, 162, 185, 195; Alaa Badaraneh / The Palestinian Museum: p. 133; Yara Bamieh: p. 169; Nadia Bseiso: p. 189; Mikaela Burstow / AAU ANASTAS: pp. 81–83, 86–87, 89, 92; Dinkum / Wikimedia Commons, Creative Commons CC0 1.0 Universal Public Domain Dedication, https://commons.wikimedia.org/wiki/File:Salvia_officinalis_serres_du_Luxembourg.jpg: p. 159 (bottom); Hareth Yousef / The Palestinian Museum: pp. 6–7, 10–11, 12–13, 19, 57, 122–23, 139, 141, 147, 149, 151 (right), 152, 153, 155, 159 (top), 180–81, 186–87, 192–93, 202 (right); Michel Écochard Archive, courtesy of Aga Khan Documentation Center, MIT Libraries (AKDC@MIT): p. 46; Ahmed Fawzy Elaraby / Alamy stock photo: p. 40 (bottom); EQRoy / Alamy stock photo: p. 33; Halim Faïdi, Maître d'Oeuvre and Architecte: p. 43; Herbert Frank / Wikimedia Commons, Creative-Commons-Lizenz Namensnennung 2.0 generisch, https://de.wikivoyage.org/wiki/Datei:Tunis,_Museum_Bardo.jpg: p. 42; Eddie Gerald / Alamy stock photo: p. 130; NasserHalaweh / Wikimedia Commons, Creative Commons Attribution-Share Alike 4.0 International license, https://commons.wikimedia.org/wiki/File:Lamiaceae_Origanum_syriacum_1_2.jpg: p. 157; Marie-Louise Halpenny / heneghan peng architects: pp. 54–55; Yara Hamdi / The Palestinian Museum: pp. 197, 206; heneghan peng architects: pp. 23, 52, 53; Alexandre Kazerouni: pp. 63, 64, 69; Sliman Mansour / The Palestinian Museum: pp. 8–9; Luis Bartolomé Marcos (LBM1948) / Wikimedia Commons, Creative Commons Attribution-Share Alike 4.0 International license, https://commons.wikimedia.org/wiki/File:Doha,_Museo_de_Arte_Isl%C3%A1mico_05.jpg: p. 34; Matson (G. Eric and Edith) Photograph Collection via the Library of Congress Prints and Photographs Division Digital ID: (digital file from original) matpc 03380 https://hdl.loc.gov/loc.pnp/matpc.03380: p. 62; Alexandre Morin Laprise / Alamy stock photo: p. 84; Dmitry Malov / iStock: p. 143 (bottom); Antonio Ottomanelli: pp. 126–27, 140, 191, 203, 204, 205, 208–09, 211, 215; The Palestinian Museum: p. 146; Dan Porges / Alamy stock photo: p. 143 (top); Rickjpelleg / Wikimedia Commons, Creative Commons Attribution 2.5 Generic, https://de.wikipedia.org/wiki/Dornige_Bibernelle#/media/Datei:Sarcopoterium_spinosum_fruit_RJP_02.jpg: p. 148 (left); Harry Rose / Wikimedia Commons, Creative Commons Attribution 2.0 Generic license, https://en.m.wikipedia.org/wiki/File:Atriplex_nummularia_-_Stem_and_leaf.jpg: p. 163; Conor Sreenan / heneghan peng architects: p. 129; Edmund Sumner / AAU ANASTAS: p. 88; TCA (Abu Dhabi Tourism & Culture Authority): p. 40 (top); Tailleurs de pierres à Jérusalem via the Library of Congress Prints and Photographs Division Digital ID: (digital file from original) ppmsca 02758 http://hdl.loc.gov/loc.pnp/ppmsca.02758: p. 79; Tarawneh / Wikimedia Commons, Creative Commons Attribution-Share Alike 3.0 Unported license, https://commons.wikimedia.org/wiki/File:Darat_Al_Funun_197.JPG: p. 37; Michael A. Toler / Aga Khan Documentation Centre: p. 35; Julia Wagner: p. 165; Welcome2Jordan: p. 151 (left); Krzysztof Ziarnek, Kenraiz / Wikimedia Commons, Creative Commons Attribution-ShareAlike 3.0 Unported, https://de.wikipedia.org/wiki/Strauch-Melde#/media/Datei:Atriplex_halimus_kz2.JPG: p. 148 (right); Zoonar GmbH, Thiago Santos / Alamy stock photo: p. 166; ZUMA Press, Inc., unknown photographer / Alamy stock photo: pp. 85, 212.

Architecture of Commonality
Grounds for Hope

Edited by Tomà Berlanda

With contributions by Nadi Abusaada, Amin Alsaden, Omar Al-Qattan, Elias and Yousef Anastas, Mirna Bamieh, Meisa Batayneh, Tomà Berlanda, Farrokh Derakhshani, Beshara Doumani, Róisín Heneghan, Walter J. Hood, Alexandre Kazerouni, Adrian Lahoud, Adila Laïdi-Hanieh, Ella Neumaier, Nabil Qaddumi, Raja Shehadeh, Cristina Steingräber, Hanan Toukan, Shadia Touqan, Sarah Zahran, and Lara Zureikat.

Editor: Tomà Berlanda

Editorial management: Ella Neumaier

Art direction: Julia Wagner, grafikanstalt

Project management: Isabelle Griffiths, Ella Neumaier, Marlene Schneider, Nadia Siméon, Cristina Steingräber

Copyediting: Dawn Michelle d'Atri

Translation from the French: John Wheelwright

Author of VOICES introductory texts and editor of interviews: Ella Neumaier

Reproductions: Eberl & Kœsel Studio GmbH, Kempten, Germany

Printing and binding: Gutenberg Beuys Feindruckerei GmbH, Langenhagen, Germany

© 2024 Aga Khan Award for Architecture, ArchiTangle GmbH, and the contributors

Aga Khan Award for Architecture
P.O. Box 2049
1211 Geneva 2
Switzerland
www.akdn.org/architecture

Published by
ArchiTangle GmbH
Meierottostrasse 1
10719 Berlin
Germany
www.architangle.com

ISBN 978-3-96680-026-6

Scan the QR codes throughout the book to access additional digital content, such as videos and architectural drawings.